The Nut Cookbook

The Nut Cookbook

William I. Kaufman

BART
NEW YORK

Reprinted by arrangement with the author

ISBN: 1-55785-084-4

First Bart Books edition: January 1989

Bart Books
155 E. 34th Street
New York, New York 10016

Manufactured in the United States of America

THE NUT COOKBOOK

is dedicated to

All the wonderful nuts that I know

CONTENTS

LIST OF RECIPES BY CATEGORY

Consult index for page numbers.

APPETIZERS & HORS D'OEUVRES

Brazil Nut Cheese Dip
Brazil Nut Clam Dip
Brazil Nut Fruited Cheese Balls
Cheese Pastry Strips
Curried Pecans
Nut Butter
(Peanut, Cashew, etc.)
Peanut Cheese Ball
Pecan Cheese Mold
Pecan Sandwich Spread
Savory Toasted Peanuts
Spiced Peanuts
Stuffed Eggs Brazilian
Toasted Brazil Nut Chips

SOUPS

Chestnut Sherry Bisque
Chicken Almond Soup
Cream of Peanut Butter Soup
Cream of Potato and Pistachio Soup
Filbert Soup
Golden Peanut Chedda Bisque
Peanut-Cress Soup Pot
Peanut Patch Corn Chowder
Swiss Chestnut Cream Soup
Turkish Almond Soup

POULTRY

Baked Chicken in Macadamia Nut Cream
Brazil Nut Chicken Oriental
Chicken Almond Pie
Chicken Pine Nut Pilaf
Chicken Queen Kapiolani
Chinese Chicken and Walnuts
Curried Turkey with Pistachios
Louisiana Roast Duck
Macadamia Nut Creamed Chicken
Quick Brazil Nut Chicken Curry

MEATS

SEAFOOD

VEGETABLES

SALADS

STUFFINGS

BREADS

DESSERTS

CAKES

PIES

COOKIES & PASTRIES

CANDIES

INTRODUCTION

In years gone by nuts were considered a luxurious accessory to festive meals. Today they are a staple food. Just add nuts and thousands of everyday recipes become a joy to the taste buds. Sprinkle them on a bowl of cream soup, toss them with your favorite salad, add them to creamed vegetables and sauce for the fish. But don't stop there. Sprinkle nuts on your ice cream, use them in croquettes, add them to stuffing for meat, fish and poultry. Try them in cooked cereal, add a handful of chopped nuts to pancake batter, stuff them into baked onions. In puddings, pies and cakes they add zing.

Each nut has its own distinctive flavor. Nuts are available to us today in dozens of varieties—shelled and unshelled, salted and plain, in bulk and in jars. There is hardly a recipe that cannot be enhanced by adding nuts in one of their many forms. Packed into each nutshell is a food of highly concentrated value, closely resembling meat. Nuts are rich in fat, rich in protein—both in proper ratio. Two Brazil nuts or five pecans or ten almonds represent about as much energy food as two slices of white bread or a cup of oatmeal. Practically all nuts contain Vitamin B_1, B_2, protein, niacin, iron and calcium.

Nuts were among the staple foods of the American Indians, although the Indian planted few, if any, trees for the purpose of crop production. The planting of nut orchards came much later. By 1900 the growing, harvesting and shelling of nuts was a large industry in the United States. Among the first planted for market were the paper-shell or Persian walnuts.

Imported seeds planted in the eastern part of the United States in the eighteenth century and on the West Coast by the Franciscan monks with the establishment of the missions have grown into a big business—a business that makes available to the American homemaker a supply of goodies to enhance the taste and eye appeal of foods at meal and treat time both. Nuts add festivity to every occasion. Each nut has its own story, its own taste. It is my hope that this cookbook will help every reader find ways of introducing the lusciousness of nuts to all who come to share the festive board.

NUT PREPARATION

Almonds are easily shelled by a twist of the fingers.

Brazil Nuts If placed in the freezer several hours before cracking, the kernel may be easily removed.

Filberts Gently strike with a hammer in center of rounded side.

Peanuts Same as for almonds.

Pecans To remove nutmeats whole, cover nuts with boiling water and let stand until cold.

Walnuts (Black or California) To remove nutmeats whole, strike with a hammer or tool in center of rounded side halfway between joining of the two halves.

GENERAL:

To chop nuts: Place nuts in wooden bowl and chop with vegetable-chopping knife.

To grind nuts: Use meat grinder or electric blender.

To slice nuts: A sharp knife is all that is needed. Brazil nuts should be boiled 3 minutes before slicing.

To shred nuts: A vegetable-shredding knife is best, but any sharp knife will do.

To toast chopped nuts: Chopped nuts to be toasted should be chopped medium fine rather than ground. Spread chopped nuts over bottom of baking dish or sheet and set in a moderate oven (350°), stirring frequently until nuts are golden brown. Remove at once and transfer them onto a cold, dry baking sheet. Any kind of nut may be prepared in this way.

To blanch nuts: Cover the nuts with boiling water and allow to stand 2 or 3 minutes. Drain, put in cold water, rub off the skins and dry on clean towels.

To blanch filberts: Cover with boiling water, let stand 6 or 7 minutes, drain, remove skins with a sharp knife.

To improve the flavor of nutmeats, especially in summer, a little heating will help. Sprinkle a thin layer of nuts on a baking sheet and heat them for 5 minutes in a moderate oven (350°). Cool before using.

Almonds, hazelnuts and other thick-skinned nuts must be blanched before they are roasted and salted.

Any nut may be glazed. Just dip in a syrup which is cooked over a low fire so that it will not caramelize too much. If glazed nuts are to be used for gifts, they should be packed between layers of wax paper in tin or airtight containers. Do not pack with other candies because they absorb moisture and will become sticky.

Frying-pan roasting: To roast pecans, walnuts, almonds and filberts combine whole nutmeat halves with 2 teaspoons of vegetable oil and 1 teaspoon salt for each cup of nutmeats. Place over a low heat, stirring constantly, until hot through. Avoid overcooking. Nutmeats, particularly pecans, darken a little more after being removed from the heat, and become crisper when they cool. Drain on absorbent paper. Blanched almonds or blanched raw peanuts may be roasted similarly, but they must be heated a little longer until light brown in color.

Oven roasting: Combine nutmeats with 2 teaspoons vegetable oil or butter, one teaspoon salt for each cup of nutmeats. Spread in a single layer in a shallow pan. Heat in a 375° oven, stirring frequently, until hot through. Drain on absorbent paper. Almonds and peanuts must be heated a little longer than other nuts.

How many nuts? One pound of unshelled almonds yields about one cup of shelled nuts. One pound of filberts yields about 1⅓ cups of nuts. One pound of peanuts yields about 2 cups of nuts. One pound of pecans yields about 1⅓ cups of nuts. One pound of California walnuts yields about 1½ cups of nuts. One pound of black walnuts yields about ½ cup of nuts.

To shell chestnuts: The easiest way is: Cut a gash on the flat side of the nut. Melt teaspoon of butter in a heavy frying pan, add the nuts and shake over a low fire about five minutes. Let cool and remove skins with a sharp knife.

For purée of chestnuts: Boil in lightly salted water until tender enough to mash.

ALMONDS

THE ALMOND

'he very name "almond" conjures the most romantic as-ects of life. We say of a luscious beauty, "She has a skin of oney and almonds" or we describe that rare contour of eye s the "almond" shape.

Mentioned in the Old Testament seventy-three times, the lmond, resembling the peach in manner of growth and ap-earance of blossom, has long been prized for its flavor and ersatility. In the days of Jacob it was an important product f commerce and was carried from Syria and Israel to Egypt, he Aegeans, and westward. Although it is native to these ountries surrounding the Mediterranean, it is not known whether it ever grew wild there. In Israel this tree blossoms s early as the month of January and is known by the name 'awakening." According to legend, such a plant budded and fruited in the tabernacle in one day after Aaron, the high priest, held it as a rod. The rod, being preserved, reached Rome to become the staff of the pope. Throughout Tuscany in Italy the branches of the almond were used as divining rods to seek out hidden treasure.

Almonds have been eaten plain and candied since the "Greek nut" was introduced into Roman life. As early as 300 B.C. Theophrastus mentioned the almond as unique be-cause it produced its blossoms before its leaves.

Brought to America from Spain by the Franciscan fathers about 1769, during the mission era, the tree was noticed by the forty-niners of the gold rush because of its loveliness.

Some of the adventurers who stayed to cultivate the Ca fornia land began the search for varieties of almond suitab to local soil and water conditions. Originally grown on slope carefully planted in summer, pruned faithfully so that su light could reach every part of the tree, the almond began t flourish until the momentous days when August Timoth Hatch succeeded in developing the Ne Plus Ultra and th now famous Nonpareil, still considered to be the best al purpose almond produced in the world.

But even after these discoveries, Americans continued t import a supply of almonds from Europe amounting t $900,000.00 in the year 1893. Domestic growers, sufferin from such oppressive competition, decided to band togethe in their search for better quality, improved techniques an equipment and more widespread markets. Concentrating o the six most promising varieties out of the more than sevent then in cultivation, they succeeded to such a great degree tha today 110,000 acres in California are covered with the delicat pink-and-white beauty of the almond blossom.

The yearly cycle of this treat begins as soon as the pre vious season's matured crop is off the trees. The ground is irrigated and disced, the trees are carefully pruned to maintain the vaselike appearance and shape, the orchard is tidied, a cover crop is planted, and insect infestation is prevented by immediate removal of all debris around the tree. In early February and March the blossoms arrive, bringing their soft, light perfume to the winds. Every device is used to guard the trees from frost damage while the bees do the work of pollinating. The almond is self-fertile and must be pollinated by trees of other almond varieties which have been planted among the main crop solely for that purpose. (In some orchards beehives exist right among the trees.) With the dropping of the "jackets" the trees are carefully tended until August, when the thin, leathery, non-edible hulls split open, exposing the nut—which does not drop to the ground, as do most other ripe fruits.

During harvesting, almonds are taken from the trees by knocking and gathering equipment, although on some ranches almonds are still jarred from the trees by hand through the use of long poles in the traditional manner.

The nuts are hulled and dried mechanically and sent in bulk for processing. They are shelled, cleaned, graded, sorted, inspected, placed in storage and finally prepared for market by blanching, roasting, shredding, chopping and slivering processes. Sold in a vast number of different quantities, these nuts are utilized in the confectionery, grocery, bakery, and ice-cream industries, and the residues are used in the making of stock feeds, charcoal briquettes, cosmetics and pharmaceuticals.

Even though the almond has become firmly entrenched in our diet in candy bars and sundaes, on coffee rings and in loose form so familiar to us all, the research to improve the quality and size of this delicacy goes on. The romance of this clean, bright tree lures men to seek ever new varieties of this nourishing epicure's delight—the almond.

CHICKEN ALMOND SOUP

1 *cup diced chicken*
½ *cup blanched almonds*
3 *cups double-strength chicken consommé*
1 *cup heavy cream*
Salt and pepper
Paprika

Combine chicken and almonds. Grind in food chopper, using fine blade. Combine consommé, cream, chicken-and-almond mixture. Season with salt and pepper to taste. Simmer in top of double boiler for 30 minutes. Serve hot. Sprinkle with paprika before serving.

Makes 4 to 6 servings.

TURKISH ALMOND SOUP

6 hard-cooked egg yolks
½ pound almonds
6 bitter almonds
1 teaspoon grated lemon rind
1 teaspoon coriander seed
4 cups veal stock
½ teaspoon salt
2 cups light cream

Place egg yolks, almonds, lemon rind and coriander seed in mortar or wooden bowl. Mix well and then pound to a paste. Mix in 1 cup of veal stock and salt. Mix well. Pour remaining veal stock in pan and bring to a boil. Add ground almond mixture. Stir well. Simmer slowly for 10 minutes. Just before serving add the cream. Reheat but do not allow to boil. Serve hot.

Makes 6 servings.

VEAL AMANDINE

1 pound veal round steak
2 tablespoons flour
1 tablespoon salad oil
Salt and pepper
½ cup dairy sour cream
¼ cup toasted blanched slivered almonds
Hot cooked noodles

Cut veal into 1½-inch squares and coat lightly with flour. Brown in hot oil. Sprinkle with salt and pepper and add hot water barely to cover meat. Cover and cook slowly 30 to 40 minutes, until meat is tender. Remove lid and allow almost all the water to evaporate. Stir in sour cream and cook slowly 5 minutes. Mix in half of almonds, and serve on hot cooked noodles (or rice) with remaining almonds sprinkled on top.

Makes 3 or 4 servings.

CHICKEN ALMOND PIE

- 1 *broiler-fryer chicken, cut in serving pieces*
- 2 *cups water*
- ½ *cup chopped celery (and a few minced leaves)*
- 1 *tablespoon instant minced onion*
- 1½ *teaspoons salt*
- 1 *4-ounce can sliced mushrooms*
- ¼ *cup butter or margarine*
- ¼ *cup flour*
- 1 *cup light cream or milk*
- ⅛ *teaspoon pepper*
- ¼ *teaspoon chopped fresh dill*
- ½ *cup toasted blanched slivered almonds*
- *Unbaked 9-inch pie crust*

In a pot slowly cook chicken, water, celery, onion, salt and liquid from mushrooms about 50 minutes, or until tender. Cool chicken and remove skin and bones, leaving meat in large pieces (about 2 cups). Melt butter and stir in flour, then cream, 1 cup stock from chicken, pepper and dill. Cook and stir until mixture is thickened and comes to a boil. Stir in chicken, mushrooms and almonds. Turn into shallow 1-quart baking dish. Top with pastry; flute and prick. Bake in a hot oven (400°) 25 to 30 minutes until golden brown.

Makes 5 or 6 servings.

ALMOND LOBSTER THERMIDOR

*4 cooked lobster tails or 2 6½-ounce cans lobster meat**
3 tablespoons butter or margarine
1 tablespoon instant minced onion
¼ cup white dinner wine or water
3 tablespoons flour
2 cups light cream
1 tablespoon chopped parsley
¾ teaspoon salt
¼ teaspoon dry mustard
Dash cayenne
¼ cup diced roasted almonds
1 cup grated Cheddar cheese
Paprika

Cut meat from lobster tails and cube. Melt butter; add onion and wine and simmer until liquid is reduced to half. Add flour and stir until smooth. Gradually add cream; continue to cook, stirring until thickened and creamy. Add parsley, salt, mustard and cayenne. Fold in cubed lobster, almonds and ½ cup cheese. Stir gently until cheese is melted. Fill lobster tails with mixture or place in 4 individual casseroles. Sprinkle with remaining cheese and paprika. Broil until cheese is melted, about 2 minutes.

Makes 4 servings.

DEVILED ALMOND CRAB

3 tablespoons butter or margarine
1 tablespoon chopped onions
¾ cup thinly sliced celery
3 tablespoons flour
1⅓ cups milk
¾ teaspoon salt
⅛ teaspoon black pepper
Dash cayenne pepper
½ teaspoon prepared mustard
¼ teaspoon Worcestershire
1 6½-ounce can crab meat or 1 cup fresh cooked crab meat
2 hard-cooked eggs
3 tablespoons chopped parsley
3 tablespoons diced pimiento
⅓ cup blanched slivered almonds

* Or use 1 pound cooked crayfish.

Melt butter and add onions and celery. Cover and cook over moderate heat about 5 minutes. Stir in flour. Add milk and seasonings, and cook and stir until thickened. Flake crab; dice eggs and add with parsley and pimiento. Heat thoroughly. Stir in almonds and serve at once.

Makes 4 servings.

TROUT AMANDINE

2 tablespoons flour
1½ teaspoons salt
¼ teaspoon pepper
2 pounds trout or fish fillets
6 tablespoons butter or margarine
¼ cup blanched slivered almonds
*3 tablespoons lemon juice**
1 tablespoon chopped parsley

Mix flour, 1 teaspoon of the salt, and pepper; sprinkle on fish. In a skillet over medium heat, fry fish in 4 tablespoons of the butter until lightly browned, about 6 minutes. Arrange fish on warmed platter. Add remaining butter to skillet and brown almonds lightly, stirring as needed. Stir in rest of salt, lemon juice and parsley and serve at once over fish.

Makes 4 to 6 servings.

ORIENTAL FILLET OF SOLE

1½ pounds sole fillets (5 or 6 medium size)
Salt
1½ cups water
2 teaspoons instant minced onion
¾ cup mayonnaise
1 tablespoon lemon juice
1 tablespoon finely chopped parsley
⅓ cup sliced unblanched almonds

Wipe fillets with damp cloth and sprinkle each side lightly with salt. Roll and skewer with toothpicks. Place rolls in fish steamer on wire rack above water; cover and steam 12 to 15

* If desired, reduce lemon juice to 1 teaspoon and add ¼ cup sherry or sauterne.

minutes, or until fillets are opaque. While fish is steaming, prepare sauce. Mix together onion, mayonnaise, lemon juice, ⅛ teaspoon salt and parsley. Carefully remove cooked fillets from steamer and quickly spread them with mayonnaise mixture. Sprinkle with almonds and serve immediately.

Makes 5 to 6 servings.

CARROT CRUNCH

- 6 *to* 8 *carrots*
- ½ *teaspoon salt*
- 1 *tablespoon butter or margarine*
- 1 *tablespoon brown sugar*
- 1 *teaspoon grated orange rind*
- ¼ *cup toasted blanched slivered almonds*

Cut carrots lengthwise into halves or quarters. Cook in small amount of water and salt until barely tender. Drain. Lift carrots out of pan and reserve. In same saucepan, stir together butter, sugar, orange rind and almonds. Return carrots to pan and simmer 5 minutes longer, turning carrots to coat with butter mixture.

Makes 4 servings.

CAULIFLOWER

- 1 10-*ounce package frozen cauliflower*
- 1 10½-*ounce can condensed cream of mushroom soup*
- ¼ *cup water*
- ¼ *cup blanched slivered almonds*

Cook cauliflower in small amount of salted water until tender. Heat mushroom soup and water; add almonds. Serve sauce over cauliflower.*

Makes 4 servings.

* Or peas, asparagus, green beans, or mixed vegetables.

SCALLOPED ONIONS

2 16-ounce cans whole baby onions
1 10½-ounce can condensed cream of celery soup
½ cup grated American cheese
¼ cup chopped or blanched slivered almonds

Drain onions and combine with soup in a casserole. Top with cheese and almonds. Bake in moderately hot oven (375°) 30 minutes.

Makes 6 servings.

BAKED SQUASH

2 cups steamed winter squash
2 tablespoons butter or margarine
2 tablespoons brown sugar
2 tablespoons cream
½ teaspoon salt
Dash ground nutmeg
1 egg, beaten
¼ cup chopped or diced roasted almonds

Mash squash. Stir in butter, sugar, cream, seasonings and egg. Fold in part of almonds, reserving a few for garnish. Pour into greased 1-quart casserole. Top with remaining almonds. Bake in moderately hot oven (375°) 25 to 30 minutes.

Makes 6 servings.

SPINACH GOURMET

2 tablespoons butter or margarine
2 tablespoons flour
1 10½-ounce can condensed chicken with rice soup
1 10-ounce package frozen chopped spinach
¼ teaspoon ground nutmeg
¼ cup diced roasted almonds
Salt

Heat butter, add flour and stir until smooth. Gradually stir in soup. Cook and stir until thickened. Add spinach and nutmeg; simmer until spinach is done (10 to 15 minutes), stirring occasionally. Add almonds and salt to taste.

Makes 4 to 6 servings.

CHINESE VEGETABLE ALMOND

2 tablespoons salad oil
½ cup thinly sliced onions
½ cup sliced mushrooms
1 cup sliced celery
1 5-ounce can sliced water chestnuts
1 cup diced cooked chicken
½ cup chicken broth
1 teaspoon cornstarch
¼ teaspoon salt
2 tablespoons cold water
1 tablespoon soy sauce
1 16-ounce can bean sprouts, drained
½ cup toasted blanched slivered almonds
Hot cooked rice

Heat oil in large frying pan. Add onions, mushrooms, celery, water chestnuts and fry lightly, cooking about 5 minutes. Add chicken and broth, cover pan, and cook slowly about 10 minutes. Combine cornstarch, salt, water and soy sauce, and stir into cooked mixture. Stir until mixture boils and thickens. Add bean sprouts and almonds. Heat, then serve at once on hot fluffy rice.

Makes 4 generous servings.

BROCCOLI WITH ALMOND SAUCE

4 tablespoons butter or margarine
2½ tablespoons flour
1¼ cups milk
¼ teaspoon salt
Dash cayenne pepper
2 egg yolks
2 tablespoons lemon juice
1½ pounds cooked broccoli or cauliflower
⅓ cup toasted blanched slivered almonds

Melt 2 tablespoons of the butter and blend in flour. Add milk, salt, and cayenne, and cook and stir until mixture is thickened and comes to a boil. Beat egg yolks lightly. Stir a little of hot sauce into yolks, then combine with remaining sauce. Cook and stir over low heat 3 or 4 minutes longer, but do not allow to boil. Stir in remaining butter, 1 tablespoon at a time. Slowly stir in lemon juice. Pour over hot cooked broccoli and sprinkle with almonds.

Makes 5 or 6 servings.

SWEET-POTATO PUFFS

3 large sweet potatoes
½ cup butter or margarine
½ cup hot milk
½ teaspoon salt
¼ cup brown sugar, firmly packed
⅛ teaspoon pumpkin-pie spice
¼ cup blanched slivered almonds

Scrub potatoes; cut off ends and place in baking pan. Bake in hot oven (400°) 1 hour. Cut potatoes lengthwise into halves and scoop pulp into a mixing bowl. Add half the butter, then milk and salt. Beat until light and fluffy. Fill shells with potato mixture; return to oven. Cream together remaining butter, sugar and pumpkin-pie spice. Fold in almonds. Place a dollop of the almond topping on each potato half. Return to oven and heat five minutes or until topping is melted.

Makes 6 servings.

GREEN BEANS AMANDINE

*2 9-ounce packages frozen cut green beans**
½ cup butter or margarine
½ cup blanched slivered almonds
¼ teaspoon salt
2 tablespoons lemon juice
Dash pepper

Cook beans as package directs; drain. Meanwhile lightly brown butter and almonds over low heat, stirring as needed. Stir in salt, lemon juice and pepper. Pour over beans; heat and serve.

Makes 6 to 8 servings.

ALMOND CRAB SALAD

1 6½-ounce can crab meat
1 hard-cooked egg
1 cup sliced celery
2 tablespoons diced pimiento
½ cup toasted blanched slivered almonds
⅓ cup mayonnaise
1 tablespoon lemon juice
½ teaspoon salt
Dash hot pepper sauce
Lettuce

Flake crab meat. Dice egg. Combine crab, egg, celery, pimiento, and almonds. Stir together mayonnaise, lemon juice, salt and hot pepper sauce. Toss with crab mixture. Serve at once on crisp lettuce.

Makes 3 or 4 servings.

* Or 2 16-ounce cans cut green beans.

CALIFORNIA ALMOND STUFFING

1 cup chopped onions
1½ cups sliced celery
1 cup butter or margarine
2 7½- to 8-ounce packages stuffing mix (4 quarts)
½ cup chopped parsley
*1 cup toasted blanched slivered almonds**
1½ cups hot giblet stock or water

Slowly cook onions and celery in butter 5 minutes, stirring occasionally. Pour over stuffing mix. Add parsley and almonds; toss lightly. Sprinkle stock on stuffing; toss again. Pack lightly into turkey.

Makes enough stuffing for 12- to 15-pound turkey.

ITALIAN MERINGUE STRIPS

3 cups sifted flour
¾ cup sugar
½ teaspoon salt
1 cup butter or margarine
2 eggs
¼ cup water
⅛ teaspoon cream of tartar
¾ cup sifted confectioners' sugar
1 teaspoon vanilla
¼ teaspoon cinnamon
3 tablespoons finely chopped candied fruits
¾ cup chopped or diced roasted almonds

Sift flour with sugar and salt. Cut in butter until mixture resembles coarse meal. Separate eggs; beat yolks lightly with water. Sprinkle over flour mixture, tossing to moisten evenly. Shape into a ball. Chill if dough is too soft for handling. Beat egg whites with cream of tartar until foamy. Gradually beat in confectioners' sugar and continue beating to stiff-peak stage. Fold in vanilla, cinnamon and candied fruits. Divide dough into 2 parts and roll each to an 8×12-inch rectangle.

* Or use diced roasted almonds.

Spread with meringue mixture, sprinkle with almonds, and cut into strips about 4×1½ inches. Place on ungreased baking sheets. Bake in moderate oven (350°) about 15 to 18 minutes, until lightly browned. Remove to wire racks to cool.

Makes about 32 bars.

PORBORONES

¾ cup toasted blanched slivered almonds
½ cup butter or margarine
1 cup sifted confectioners' sugar
½ teaspoon vanilla
1¼ cups sifted flour
¼ teaspoon salt
⅛ teaspoon cinnamon

Chop almonds. Cream butter and sugar; stir in vanilla and almonds. Sift together flour, salt and cinnamon. Stir into butter mixture. Divide dough into two parts; roll each part into a foot-long roll. Cut into ½-inch lengths and place on well-greased cooky sheet. Bake in moderately hot oven (375°) about 10 minutes or until lightly browned. Cool and store in airtight container.

Makes 4 dozen cookies.

MEXICAN TEA CAKES

1½ cups blanched whole almonds
1 cup butter or margarine
¼ cup sugar
1 teaspoon grated orange rind
1 teaspoon vanilla
¼ teapoon salt
2 cups sifted flour
Confectioners' sugar

Chop almonds fine or put through meat grinder, using medium blade. Cream butter and sugar; mix in orange rind, vanilla and salt. Stir in almonds and flour. Chill dough if too soft for easy handling. Roll dough into small balls. Place on greased cooky sheet and flatten each cooky slightly. Bake in moderately slow oven (325°) about 25 minutes. While hot, roll in confectioners' sugar. When cold, roll again in confectioners' sugar and store in airtight container.

Makes 5 dozen cookies.

DUTCH ST. NICHOLAS COOKIES

½ cup unblanched almonds
¾ cup butter or margarine
½ cup brown sugar, firmly packed
¼ teaspoon ground nutmeg
¼ teaspoon ground ginger
¼ teaspoon ground cloves
1½ teaspoons cinnamon
2 tablespoons milk
2 cups sifted flour
1½ teaspoons baking powder
½ teaspoon salt
¼ cup coarsely grated citron

Chop almonds fine or put through food chopper, using medium blade. Cream butter, sugar, spices and milk together. Sift flour with baking powder and salt. Add to creamed mixture. Add citron and almonds. Knead to make a firm ball. Chill in refrigerator. Roll dough thin on lightly floured board and cut with cooky cutter. Bake on greased cooky sheets in moderately hot oven (375°) 7 to 10 minutes.

Makes about 3½ dozen (depending upon size of cutter).

GOLDEN ANNIVERSARY FRUITCAKE

1 *cup shortening*
1 *cup sugar*
1 *teaspoon vanilla*
4 *eggs*
2½ *cups sifted flour*
1 *teaspoon baking powder*
1 *teaspoon salt*
½ *cup apricot nectar*
2 *cups blanched slivered almonds*
1 *cup golden raisins*
1 *cup halved candied cherries*
1 *cup sliced dried apricots*
1 *cup diced candied pineapple*
1 *cup shredded citron*
1 *cup candied orange peel*

Cream shortening, sugar and vanilla together. Beat in eggs one at a time. Sift flour with baking powder and salt. Blend into creamed mixture alternately with nectar. Add almonds, fruits and peels and mix well. Turn into greased and floured pans. Bake in slow oven (300°) about 2¼ to 2½ hours, or until cake tests done. Keep shallow pan of hot water on lowest shelf of oven while cake is baking. Let stand about 15 minutes, then turn cake out onto wire rack to cool.

Makes about 5 pounds cake (1 10-inch tube pan, or 2 loaves 9×5×3 inches).

LINZER TORTE

1½ cups whole almonds, unblanched
1 cup butter or margarine
1 cup sugar
2 egg yolks, beaten
1½ teaspoons grated lemon rind
2 cups sifted flour
1 tablespoon cinnamon
½ teaspoon ground cloves
1 cup raspberry jam

Grind almonds, using medium blade. Cream butter and sugar. Add egg yolks, almonds and lemon rind. Sift together flour and spices and add to creamed mixture. Knead until dough is firm and holds together. Pat two thirds of the dough into a 9-inch round cake pan, covering the bottom and sides. The layer should be about ½ inch thick. Spread with jam. Form 8 ½-inch-thick strips with remaining dough. Make lattice top by placing 4 strips one way and 4 the opposite. Bake in moderate oven (350°) 30 to 40 minutes. Cool. Cut into pie-shaped wedges 1 inch wide at the rim.

Makes about 30 pieces.

STOLLEN

1 package dry yeast
¼ cup lukewarm water
⅔ cup milk
½ cup butter or margarine
¼ cup sugar
1 egg
½ teaspoon almond extract
½ teaspoon salt
3¼ to 3½ cups sifted flour
¾ cup blanched slivered almonds
1 cup golden raisins
½ cup halved candied cherries
Confectioners'-sugar icing

Dissolve yeast in water. Scald milk; add butter and sugar nd stir until sugar is dissolved. Cool to lukewarm. Beat egg nd add to milk mixture with yeast, almond extract and alt. Stir in 2 cups of the flour and beat until smooth. Stir n almonds, raisins and cherries. Add remaining flour and nix until smooth. Cover and let rise in warm place until loubled in bulk (about 1½ hours). Punch down; knead ightly, and pat to 12-inch circle. Fold in half and press edges ogether firmly. Place on greased baking sheet. Brush top with nelted butter. Let rise ½ hour in warm place. Bake in noderate oven (350°) about 30 minutes. Spread top with cing while warm.

Makes 1 large loaf.

ALMOND CRUNCH PUMPKIN PIE

2 eggs
¾ cup sugar
1 tablespoon pumpkin-pie spice
¾ teaspoon salt
1 14½-ounce can evaporated milk
1 16-ounce can pumpkin
1 unbaked 9-inch pie shell
2 tablespoons brown sugar
1 tablespoon soft butter or margarine
½ cup blanched slivered almonds

Beat eggs with sugar. Stir in spice, salt, milk and pumpkin. 'our into pie shell and bake in hot oven (425°) 15 minutes. Reduce heat to moderate (350°) and bake 30 minutes. Combine brown sugar, butter and almonds and sprinkle over top of pie. Continue baking 15 minutes longer or until pumpkin custard is set.

Makes 6 to 8 servings.

ALMOND CHOCOLATE SOUFFLE

3 tablespoons butter or margarine
2 tablespoons flour
½ cup sugar
¼ teaspoon salt
1 cup milk
2 ounces unsweetened chocolate, grated
½ teaspoon vanilla
½ teaspoon almond extract
4 eggs, separated
½ cup diced roasted almonds

Melt butter and stir in flour. Add sugar, salt, milk and chocolate. Cook over medium low heat, stirring constantly until thickened. Remove from heat; add vanilla and almond extract. Beat egg whites until stiff; with same beater beat egg yolks. Stir yolks into chocolate mixture; fold in egg whites and almonds. Turn into well-greased 1-quart soufflé dish or casserole. Bake in hot oven (400°) 15 minutes. Reduce the temperature to moderate (350°) and continue to bake 20 to 25 minutes. Serve immediately. If desired, serve with a thin custard sauce, whipped cream or ice cream.

Makes 4 to 6 servings.

ALMOND STRAWBERRY TRIFLE

1 package vanilla pudding mix (regular, not instant)
1½ cups milk
Dash salt
⅓ cup orange juice or white dinner wine
20 lady fingers
½ cup toasted slivered blanched almonds
¼ cup strawberry jelly
1 cup heavy cream
Additional almonds for garnish
Fresh strawberries or strawberry jelly

Prepare pudding mix as package directs, using only 1½ ups milk and salt. Remove from heat and add ¼ cup orange iice. Chill. Arrange lady fingers over bottom and around sides f 8-inch spring-form pan or serving dish. Sprinkle with re-naining orange juice and the almonds. Spoon on jelly. Pour hilled pudding over jelly; refrigerate several hours. Whip ream and spread over top of pudding. Garnish with additi-onal almonds and fresh strawberries or dollops of strawberry elly, if desired.

Makes 6 to 8 servings.

HOLIDAY CANDY SLICES

1 *cup sugar*
1 *cup brown sugar, firmly packed*
¾ *cup water*
¼ *teaspoon cream of tartar*
1 *teaspoon vanilla*
¾ *cup diced roasted almonds*

Combine sugars, water and cream of tartar and stir over ow heat until sugar is dissolved. Heat to boiling, cover and oil slowly 3 or 4 minutes to dissolve any crystals on sides f pan. Uncover and boil without stirring to medium-hard all (242°). Pour out at once onto platter which has been nsed in cold water. Allow to cool until barely warm. Add anilla and stir until creamy. Shape with hands into two rolls, inch in diameter. Roll each in almonds, wrap in wax paper nd allow to set until firm. Cut into slices with sharp knife.

Makes about 1½ pounds.

SNOWTOPS

½ cup sugar
1/16 teaspoon cream of tartar
¼ cup hot water
½ teaspoon vanilla
Drop or two mint extract
1¼ cups sifted confectioners' sugar
2 cups whole unblanched roasted almonds

Combine sugar, cream of tartar and hot water in smal saucepan. Cook over low heat until sugar dissolves. Continu cooking to 226° on a candy thermometer, or to a thin syrup Cool to lukewarm. Stir in flavorings and confectioners' suga Hold almonds one at a time by the pointed end and di rounded end into sugar mixture. Place on wax paper t harden.

Makes about 1¼ pounds.

ALMOND PANOCHA

3 cups brown sugar, firmly packed
⅛ teaspoon salt
1 cup milk
2 tablespoons light corn syrup
2 tablespoons butter or margarine
1 teaspoon vanilla
1 cup toasted slivered almonds

In saucepan combine sugar, salt, milk and syrup. Cook ove low heat, stirring constantly until sugar is dissolved. Bo gently, stirring often to 236° or until a little mixture forn a soft ball in cold water. Remove from heat, add butter an cool without stirring. Add vanilla. Beat until creamy and n longer shiny. Stir in almonds and pour into buttered 8-inc square pan. Cool and cut into squares.

Makes 36 squares.

CALIFORNIA ALMOND NOUGAT

2 cups sugar
1 cup light corn syrup
½ cup water
2 egg whites
3 tablespoons soft butter or margarine
2 teaspoons vanilla
1 cup golden raisins
1 cup diced roasted almonds

Combine sugar, syrup and water in saucepan and cook over w heat, stirring until sugar is dissolved. Cover and cook out 5 minutes, to dissolve any sugar crystals on sides of n. Uncover and boil to hard-ball stage (250°). Beat egg hites until stiff, and gradually pour about half of hot syrup er them, beating continuously. Return remaining syrup to at, and boil to hard-crack stage (300°). Pour over first mixre, beating again. Continue beating until thick. Stir in but-, vanilla, raisins and almonds. Turn into lightly buttered inch square pan. Allow to set thoroughly. Cut into squares, d wrap individually in wax paper.

Makes about 2 pounds.

YULETIDE CANDY ROUNDS

¾ cup diced roasted almonds
1½ cups sugar
½ cup brown sugar, firmly packed
¾ cup water
¼ teaspoon cream of tartar
1 teaspoon vanilla
¼ cup diced candied fruits

With a rolling pin, crush almonds. In a saucepan, comne sugars, water and cream of tartar; bring to a boil, stirring til sugar is dissolved. Cover and boil 3 minutes to dissolve y crystals on sides of pan. Uncover; boil without stirring to medium-hard-ball stage (242°). Pour onto platter whic has been rinsed in cold water. Allow to cool until barel warm. Add vanilla and stir until creamy. Quickly stir i candied fruit and shape with hands into two rolls 1 inch i diameter. Roll each in almonds, wrap in wax paper and a low to set until firm. Slice with sharp knife.

Makes 1½ pounds.

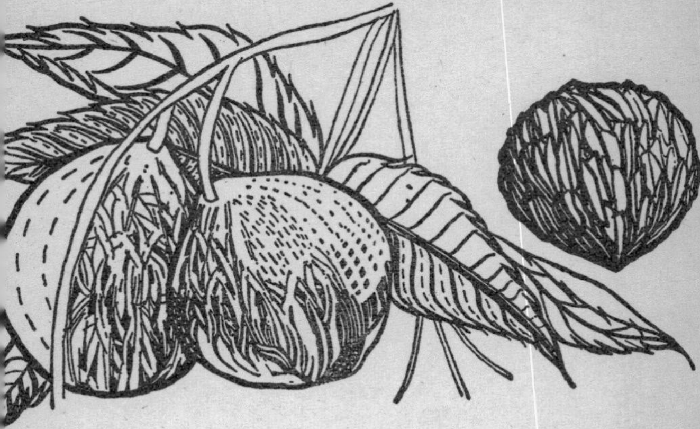

BLACK WALNUTS

THE BLACK WALNUT

The black walnut differs in size, shape, color and flavor from the California walnut we know so well. Once one of the best-known and most broadly distributed trees in our land, the black walnut is often considered to be the national tree of America. Great numbers of these giants were felled for timber during the settling of the frontier, though some few were left standing for their ornamental beauty.

The black walnut belongs to the hickory family, as does the pecan. The trees grow to an immense size, and the dark-colored wood has been much prized for handsome cabinet-work. The husks of the fruit are thin and roughly dotted, while the wild nut has a hard, thick, deep, unevenly corrugated shell. (Today's cultivated varieties, notably the Thomas, have a fairly thin shell which is reasonably easy to crack.)

To the American Indian the black walnut offered a very important source of food, and in the hard, aromatic husks he found the means for dyeing cloth and tanning skins.

Today's American finds the flavor of this native nut strong and pungent. It is a flavor which is not lost in cooking, and in fact its over-strong qualities are gently subdued by heat, so that it is especially desirable in dishes that require long hours of preparation.

The kernels of the black walnut are of good quality and high nutritional value, and their very special taste puts them in great demand for use in casseroles, candies, baked goods, and ice creams.

BANANA AND BLACK WALNUT SALAD

- *½ pound cream cheese*
- *2 tablespoons mayonnaise*
- *2 tablespoons lemon juice*
- *1 teaspoon salt*
- *1 cup crushed, drained pineapple*
- *3 mashed bananas*
- *¼ cup maraschino cherries, chopped*
- *½ cup chopped black walnuts*
- *½ cup heavy cream, whipped*

Beat together the cream cheese, mayonnaise, lemon juice and salt. Add fruit and black walnuts and fold in the whipped cream. Turn into molds and chill until firm.

Makes 6 servings.

BLACK WALNUT FRUIT BREAD

- *½ cup boiling water*
- *2 tablespoons butter or margarine*
- *2 tablespoons grated orange rind*
- *⅓ cup orange juice*
- *½ cup raisins or finely cut dates*
- *1 cup sugar*
- *1 teaspoon vanilla*
- *1 egg, slightly beaten*
- *½ cup coarsely chopped black walnuts*
- *2 cups sifted flour*
- *¼ teaspoon soda*
- *2 teaspoons baking powder*
- *½ teaspoon salt*

In a mixing bowl put water, butter, orange rind, orange juice, raisins or dates, sugar, vanilla, egg and black walnuts. Sift in flour, soda, baking powder and salt. Mix well. Pour batter into greased 8½×4½×3-inch loaf pan. Bake in a moderate oven (350°) 1 hour or until done. Remove from pan; cool on wire rack.

Makes 1 loaf.

BLACK WALNUT CRUMB CAKE

½ cup coarsely chopped black walnuts
½ cup brown sugar, firmly packed
1 tablespoon flour
1 teaspoon cinnamon
5 tablespoons butter or margarine
1 cup sugar
2 eggs
1½ cups sifted flour
2 teaspoons baking powder
¼ teaspoon salt
½ cup milk

Combine black walnuts, brown sugar, flour and cinnamon. Melt 1 tablespoon of the butter; stir into black-walnut mixture. Mix well; reserve. Cream remaining 4 tablespoons butter; add sugar and cream well. Beat in eggs one at a time. Sift together flour, baking powder and salt; add alternately with milk to creamed mixture. Turn into 12 greased 2½-inch muffin pans; sprinkle nut mixture over top. Bake in a moderately hot oven (375°) 25 minutes.

Makes 12 coffee cakes.

BLACK WALNUT CINNAMON STICKS

1 loaf unsliced bread
⅔ cup evaporated milk
4 tablespoons melted butter
2 tablespoons cinnamon
6 tablespoons sugar
6 tablespoons ground toasted black walnuts

Cut 6 1-inch slices from loaf of bread. Remove crusts; cut each slice into 3 strips. Dip strips into evaporated milk; brush with melted butter. Combine cinnamon, sugar and black walnuts; roll strips in mixture. Place on rack in shallow baking pan. Bake in hot oven (400°) 20 minutes.

Makes 18 strips or 6 servings.

APPLE SAUCE NUT CAKE

2 cups sugar
1 cup shortening
2½ cups apple sauce
4 cups sifted flour
3 teaspoons soda
1 teaspoon cinnamon
1 teaspoon nutmeg
½ teaspoon ground cloves
1 pound raisins
1 cup chopped black walnuts

Cream sugar and shortening, and add apple sauce. Sift together flour, soda, cinnamon, nutmeg, cloves and add to shortening mixture. Stir raisins and nuts into creamed mixture, using part of flour to dredge raisins and nuts. Bake in 9×13-inch pan in moderately slow oven (325°) for 75 minutes.

Makes 1 loaf cake.

BLACK WALNUT FRUITCAKE

1 cup black walnuts
1 cup raisins
1 3½-ounce can flaked coconut
1½ cups sugar
1 cup butter or margarine
1 cup blackberry jam
2 eggs, well beaten
3 cups sifted flour
1 teaspoon soda
1 tablespoon allspice
1 cup buttermilk

Put black walnuts, raisins and coconut through food chopper. Cream together sugar, butter and jam. Add eggs, half at a time. Sift together flour, soda and allspice. Add alternately to creamed mixture with buttermilk. Turn into a 9-inch tube pan. Bake in a moderate oven (350°) 1 hour.

Makes 1 9-inch cake.

NUT CAKE

1½ cups sugar
½ cup shortening
2 cups sifted cake flour
2 teaspoons baking powder
1 cup milk
1 teaspoon vanilla
4 egg whites
1 cup black walnuts

Cream sugar and shortening. Sift together flour and baking powder. Add alternately with milk to creamed mixture. Add vanilla. Fold in egg whites, beaten stiff. Fold in black walnuts, stirring as little as possible. Turn into 2 greased 9-inch cake pans, lined with wax paper. Bake in a moderate oven (350°), 25–30 minutes. When cool, frost with confectioners'-sugar frosting.

Makes 1 9-inch layer cake.

PINEAPPLE WALNUT COOKIES

½ cup shortening
½ cup sugar
½ cup brown sugar, firmly packed
1 egg
½ cup crushed pineapple
2 cups sifted flour
¼ teaspoon salt
¼ teaspoon soda
2 teaspoons baking powder
1 teaspoon lemon extract
⅔ cup chopped black walnuts

Cream shortening, sugars, and egg. Add pineapple, then flour sifted with salt, soda and baking powder. Add flavoring and chopped walnuts. Drop by teaspoonfuls on greased cooky sheet and flatten with the bottom of a glass dipped in sugar. Bake in moderate oven (350°) about 12 minutes.

Makes 5 dozen cookies.

REFRIGERATOR COOKIES

1 cup sugar
1 cup brown sugar, firmly packed
1½ cups shortening
3 eggs, well beaten
1 cup chopped black walnuts
1 teaspoon salt
4½ cups sifted flour
2 teaspoons soda
1 teaspoon cinnamon
½ teaspoon nutmeg
½ teaspoon cloves

Cream sugars and shortening. Add eggs and mix thoroughly. Add nuts, then dry ingredients sifted together. Shape into a roll, place in refrigerator overnight. Cut ¼ inch thick. Place on cooky sheet and bake in hot oven (425°) for 8 minutes.

Makes 6 dozen cookies.

BLACK WALNUT COOKIES

¾ cup shortening
2 cups brown sugar, firmly packed
2 eggs, beaten
1 cup chopped black walnuts
1 teaspoon vanilla
3 cups sifted flour
½ teaspoon salt
½ teaspoon soda
⅓ cup condensed milk

Cream shortening and sugar. Add eggs, black walnuts and vanilla. Fold in flour, salt and soda. Add milk and mix thoroughly. Drop by teaspoonfuls on greased cooky sheet and bake in moderately hot oven (375°) about 15 minutes.

Makes 5 dozen cookies.

BLACK WALNUT APPLE SAUCE COOKIES

½ cup butter
1 cup brown sugar, firmly packed
1 egg
1 cup apple sauce
1 cup raisins
1 cup chopped black walnuts
2 cups sifted flour
1 teaspoon soda
½ teaspoon ground cloves
½ teaspoon cinnamon
½ teaspoon salt
½ teaspoon nutmeg

Cream butter and sugar. Blend in egg and apple sauce. Add raisins and walnuts to flour which has been sifted with soda and spices, then add to creamed mixture. Drop by teaspoonfuls on greased cooky sheet. Bake in moderate oven (350°) for 12 to 18 minutes.

Makes 4 dozen cookies.

BLACK WALNUT PIE

½ cup butter
1 cup sugar
3 slightly beaten eggs
¾ cup dark corn syrup
¼ teaspoon salt
1 teaspoon vanilla
1 cup black walnuts

Prepare pastry for 9-inch pie shell. Cream butter, add sugar gradually and cream together until light and fluffy. Add remaining ingredients and blend well. Pour into pastry shell. Bake on lower shelf in moderately hot oven (375°) 40 to 45 minutes. Cool and cut into small servings. Rich but good.

Makes 1 9-inch pie.

NUT KISSES

1/8 teaspoon salt
2 egg whites
1 cup sugar
1/2 teaspoon vanilla
1 tablespoon flour
1 cup broken black walnuts

Add salt to egg whites and beat until they hold a peak. Then add sugar very slowly. Beating constantly, add vanilla and fold in the flour and nuts. Drop by teaspoonfuls onto greased and lightly floured cooky sheet and bake in moderately slow oven (325°) 10 minutes.

Makes 2 dozen kisses.

BRAZIL NUTS

THE BRAZIL NUT

This nut, which grows in the Amazon jungle, is called in its native country the *castanha-do-Pará,* chestnut of Pará. The tree on which this nut grows is a handsome one, growing entirely wild in groves. Unique in appearance, it has a tall, straight, 150-foot-high trunk and fanned-out upper section of branches that tower above the jungle. Its flowers, which blossom in creamy white clusters, appear somewhere from October to March, and fourteen months later the fruits appear. What a strange and wondrous sight to see the tree bearing fresh blossoms even before the previous year's nuts have fallen! This occurs when the tree is five years old. Fruit appears when it is eight years old, and at twelve the tree begins to give maximum production. Its lifetime yield has been determined at an average 500–1000 pounds of nuts, weight of the pod excluded.

Gathering Brazil nuts is a dangerous occupation. The Amazon River forms the great highway for the Brazil-nut trade, and the gatherers, called *castanheiros,* must depend on enough rainfall to permit navigation of the streams that penetrate the jungles. The *castanheiro* goes inland in winter. He lives in the area where he does his work, sleeping in rough shelters, living off nature. Each day he risks his life, for should one of the three- to four-pound pods, which bear a shell thick and hard as the hardest of woods, strike him, falling from 100 feet, the blow would be forceful enough to cause instant death. Gatherers therefore do not go under the trees when there is wind, and generally confine their work to the hours before midday when the danger is minimal.

The *castanheiros* use their machetes to tap three or four smart blows on the weakest part of the pods (*ouricos*), which are generally opened right in the jungle on the spot where they are gathered. Inside each pod, sectioned as in a grapefruit, lie twelve to twenty of the now familiar three-sided seeds we know as Brazil nuts. The nuts are placed in rattan baskets and the baskets are dipped in the stream so that all extraneous matter falls away. Then they are taken to a central gathering point, called a *barração*, located along the stream where they are transferred to motor boats or river steamers and taken to the ports of Pará and Manáos. Handled in bulk in shell, nuts are stored in barges and later placed on ocean steamers to be carried to the world markets. In transit they are ventilated and turned regularly to facilitate drying. Shelled nuts for use in candy manufacture, baking, and the nut-salting industry are graded according to size and canned for exportation. Those to be purchased by consumers may be found in every kind of retail food outlet. They are easy to slice, grind and chop, and when used in a cake batter their extremely high oil content prevents the drying of the finished product for as long as ten days.

Originally introduced to Boston by the seagoing masters of the Yankee clipper ships, Brazil nuts have indeed made a long journey from the days when these choice tidbits were eagerly sought in the toe of the Christmas stocking to today, when their popularity makes them the first to disappear from the nut bowl. No wonder the Brazil nut is called "the king of nuts."

BRAZIL NUT CHEESE DIP

3 *ounces Roquefort or blue cheese*
2 *tablespoons medium-dry white wine*
¼ *cup finely chopped Brazil nuts*

Allow cheese to soften at room temperature. Cream and blend cheese with wine; add nuts. Serve with Cheese Pastry Strips.

Makes ⅔ cup.

CHEESE PASTRY STRIPS

½ package (1 cup) pie crust mix
¼ cup grated sharp Cheddar cheese
¼ cup very finely chopped Brazil nuts

Prepare pastry as directed on package, adding cheese and Brazil nuts before stirring in water. Roll into 12×6-inch rectangle; cut lengthwise into ½-inch strips; cut each strip in half. Bake on ungreased cooky sheet in moderate oven (350°) 20 minutes.

Makes 48 strips.

BRAZIL NUT FRUITED CHEESE BALLS

1 *3-ounce package cream cheese*
¼ cup well-drained crushed pineapple
¼ cup finely chopped Brazil nuts
Pretzel sticks

Cream the chesse until smooth, add pineapple and blend. Form into ½-inch balls; roll in chopped Brazil nuts. Chill. Pierce each ball with a pretzel stick. Serve on hors d'oeuvre tray.

Makes 24 hors d'oeuvres.

NOTE: Larger balls (1-inch) may be served to garnish a luncheon fruit salad.

STUFFED EGGS BRAZILIAN

6 hard-cooked eggs
½ cup very finely chopped Brazil nuts
2 teaspoons vinegar
⅛ teaspoon dry mustard
½ teaspoon salt
½ teaspoon Worcestershire sauce
⅛ teaspoon hot pepper sauce
2 tablespoons mayonnaise

Cut eggs into halves. Remove yolks and put through a sieve, or mash with a fork. Combine yolks with remaining ingredients and blend. Fill egg-white halves. Serve as hors d'oeuvres or as a salad.

Makes 12 stuffed eggs.

BRAZIL NUT CLAM DIP

1 3-ounce package cream cheese
1/16 teaspoon curry powder
1 10-ounce can minced clams
¼ cup finely chopped Brazil nuts

Blend cream cheese and curry powder. Drain clams well and add to cream cheese; mix thoroughly. Stir in Brazil nuts. Turn into serving dish and serve with crisp crackers.

Makes approximately 1 cup.

NOTE: Clam juice drained from clams may be used in equal parts with tomato or grapefruit juice as cocktail.

TOASTED BRAZIL NUT CHIPS

1½ cups shelled Brazil nuts
2 tablespoons butter or margarine
1 teaspoon salt

Cover nuts with cold water. Bring slowly to a boil. Simmer to 3 minutes. Drain and cut lengthwise into thin slices bout ⅛ inch thick. Spread out in shallow pan. Dot with utter; sprinkle with salt. Bake in a moderate oven (350°) 12 o 15 minutes, stirring occasionally.

Makes approximately 2 cups.

BRAZIL NUT-STUFFED MUSHROOMS

1 pound large mushrooms
⅓ cup packaged seasoned dry bread crumbs
¼ teaspoon salt
¼ cup chopped Brazil nuts
2 teaspoons capers
3 tablespoons butter

Wash mushrooms. Remove stems; chop fine. Combine with bread crumbs, salt, Brazil nuts and capers. Spoon Brazil nut mixture into caps. Place in greased shallow baking pan. Dot each mushroom with butter. Bake in moderate oven (350°) 20 to 25 minutes. Serve on saffron rice.

Makes 4 to 6 servings.

GLAZED ONIONS WITH BRAZIL NUTS

2 dozen small onions (about 1½ pounds)
3 tablespoons butter or margarine
½ cup sliced Brazil nuts
1 tablespoon sugar
¾ teaspoon salt
⅛ teaspoon pepper

Peel onions; place in baking dish with remaining ingredients. Cover; bake in moderate oven (350°) 1 hour, or until onions are tender. Stir once after first 15 minutes of baking.

Makes 6 servings.

BRAZIL NUT CHICKEN ORIENTAL

2 tablespoons salad oil
¾ cup coarsely chopped Brazil nuts
1 cup diced celery
2 cups chicken stock
1 10-ounce package frozen julienne green beans
1 16-ounce can bean sprouts, drained
1 can (3 or 4 ounces) sliced mushrooms
2 cups diced cooked chicke
1 teaspoon monosodium glutamate
1 tablespoon soy sauce
½ teaspoon ginger
1 tablespoon cornstarch
¼ cup water
2 scallions, sliced (optional)
1 cup shredded lettuce

Heat oil in large skillet. Add Brazil nuts and cook, stirrin occasionally, until lightly browned. Add celery; cook unt tender, but not brown. Add chicken stock, beans, bea sprouts, mushrooms, chicken, monosodium glutamate, so sauce and ginger. Bring to a boil, breaking up frozen bear with a fork. Reduce heat and simmer 5 minutes. Mix to gether cornstarch and water; stir to smooth paste. Graduall add to chicken mixture and cook, stirring constantly, unt mixture comes to a boil. Add scallions and lettuce; cook minutes longer. Serve with hot cooked rice.

Makes 6 servings.

QUICK BRAZIL NUT CHICKEN CURRY

4 tablespoons butter or margarine
¼ cup finely minced onions
¼ cup diced celery
4 tablespoons flour
2 teaspoons curry powder
⅛ teaspoon ginger
1 teaspoon salt
1 can (3 or 4 ounces) sliced mushrooms
Milk
1 6-ounce can chicken
2 hard-cooked eggs, quartered
½ teaspoon lemon juice
3 cups hot cooked rice
½ cup sliced toasted Brazi nuts

Melt butter; add onions and celery and cook until tender ut not brown. Add flour, curry powder, ginger and salt; stir o a smooth paste. Drain mushrooms and reserve liquid; add nilk to make 2 cups. Add to flour mixture and cook, stirring onstantly, until mixture thickens and comes to a boil. Dice hicken; add to hot mixture with mushrooms, eggs and lemon uice. Heat to serving temperature. To serve, put rice in border on platter and chicken mixture in center; sprinkle with liced Brazil nuts.

Makes 4 servings.

BRAZIL NUT CRAB MEAT SALAD

1 *6½-ounce can crab meat*
½ *cup diced celery*
½ *cup sliced Brazil nuts*
2 *tablespoons chili sauce*
⅓ *cup mayonnaise*
1 *tablespoon lemon juice*
¼ *teaspoon salt*
Avocado or tomato

Shred crab meat and remove membrane; add celery and Brazil nuts. Combine chili sauce, mayonnaise, lemon juice and salt. Add to salad mixture and mix lightly. Serve with avocado or tomato wedges.

Makes 4 servings.

GLAZED PEACHES WITH BRAZIL NUTS

1 *29-ounce can cling peach halves*
2 *tablespoons lemon juice*
½ *teaspoon grated lemon rind*
½ *cup chopped Brazil nuts*
2 *tablespoons brown sugar*

Drain peach syrup into saucepan; boil rapidly until reduced to 1 cup. Remove from heat; add lemon juice and rind. Put peach halves in shallow baking dish, hollow side up; sprinkle with nuts and brown sugar. Spoon over peach-lemon syrup. Bake in moderate oven (350°) 25 to 30 minutes, basting occasionally. Serve as a meat garnish, chilled as a dessert with ice cream, or in a fruit salad platter.

Makes 4 to 6 servings.

BRAZIL NUT STUFFING

- *2 tablespoons butter*
- *½ cup chopped Brazil nuts*
- *2 tablespoons chopped onions*
- *¼ cup diced celery with leaves*
- *½ teaspoon monosodium glutamate*
- *½ teaspoon salt*
- *⅛ teaspoon hot pepper sauce*
- *¼ teaspoon poultry seasoning*
- *2 cups lightly packed bread crumbs or cubes*
- *1 tablespoon chopped parsley*
- *2 tablespoons boiling water or stock*

Melt butter in saucepan or skillet. Add Brazil nuts, onions, celery, monosodium glutamate, salt, hot pepper sauce and poultry seasoning. Cook until Brazil nuts are lightly browned. Add to bread crumbs and parsley. Add water or stock, toss lightly with a fork until well mixed. Sprinkle cavity of bird with additional monosodium glutamate before stuffing lightly.

Makes 3 cups.

BAKED APPLES CANTON WITH BRAZIL NUT-FRUIT CENTERS

- *6 large baking apples*
- *1 cup coarsely chopped Brazil nuts*
- *½ cup chopped pitted dates*
- *⅓ cup chopped candied ginger*
- *1 cup light corn syrup*
- *1 teaspoon powdered ginger*
- *Red food coloring*
- *Sugar*

Core apples almost through. Pare about ⅓ of the way down from stem end. Combine Brazil nuts, dates and candied ginger. Fill centers of apples with nut-fruit mixture. Combine corn syrup and powdered ginger. Tint red with food coloring; simmer 5 minutes. Brush apples thickly with this mixture. Place in baking dish; add enough boiling water to cover bottom of baking dish; bake in moderate oven (350°) about 40 minutes or until tender, basting frequently with the syrup. Remove from oven. Sprinkle with sugar; broil with surface of apples 4 inches below source of heat, basting with remaining syrup and sprinkling with additional sugar, until glazed, about 15 minutes.

Makes 6 servings.

BRAZIL NUT PLANTATION PUDDING

2¼ cups sifted flour
¾ cup sugar
¾ teaspoon nutmeg
1½ teaspoons cinnamon
½ teaspoon salt
½ cup shortening
½ cup finely chopped Brazil nuts
1 cup unsulphured molasses
1 cup cold water
1 teaspoon soda
2 3-ounce packages cream cheese
2 tablespoons milk

Sift together flour, sugar, nutmeg, cinnamon and salt. Add shortening; cut with two knives or pastry blender until mixture resembles coarse crumbs. Stir in nuts. Combine unsulphured molasses, water and soda. Alternate crumbs and liquid in a greased 8×8×2-inch square pan, beginning and ending with crumbs. Stir gently only 2 or 3 times with a fork. Bake in a moderate oven (350°) 1 hour. When ready to serve, blend together cream cheese and milk. Cut cake into squares; place spoonful cream cheese topping on each square. Top each serving with Lemon Sauce.

Makes 9 servings.

LEMON SAUCE

2 tablespoons cornstarch
½ cup sugar
¼ teaspoon salt
2 cups boiling water
3 tablespoons lemon juice
1 tablespoon grated lemon rind
¼ cup butter or margarine

Mix together cornstarch, sugar and salt in saucepan. Gradually stir in boiling water. Cook, stirring constantly, until mixture boils and is thickened and clear. Remove from heat; stir in remaining ingredients. Serve warm.

Makes 2¼ cups.

BRAZIL NUT PLUM PUDDING

½ cup orange juice
1¾ cups seedless raisins
⅓ cup diced citron
1 apple, peeled and chopped
1 tablespoon grated orange rind
2 eggs, slightly beaten
½ cup unsulphured molasses
1 cup chopped Brazil nuts
½ cup (2 ounces) ground suet
¾ cup dry bread crumbs
½ cup sifted flour
1 teaspoon baking powder
½ teaspoon soda
¼ cup sugar
½ teaspoon salt
½ teaspoon cinnamon
¼ teaspoon allspice
¼ teaspoon ground cloves

Pour orange juice over raisins, citron, apple and orange rind; let stand 1 hour. Combine eggs and molasses; stir in Brazil nuts, suet and bread crumbs. Sift in remaining ingredients; blend well. Add fruit mixture; mix well. Turn into a greased 2-quart pudding mold with a tight-fitting cover. Or cover with aluminum foil and tie securely. Place on rack in deep kettle; pour in boiling water to half the depth of the mold. Cover and steam 5 hours, adding more boiling water during steaming if necessary. Serve warm with softened ice cream or pudding sauce.

Makes 12 servings.

BRAZIL NUT-CHERRY LOAF

1 cup very finely chopped Brazil nuts
½ cup very finely chopped candied cherries
¼ cup very finely chopped candied pineapple
3 egg whites
¼ cup sugar
1½ cups sifted flour
2 teaspoons baking powder
¾ teaspoon salt
⅔ cup sugar
½ cup shortening
⅔ cup milk
1 teaspoon almond flavoring

Prepare Brazil nuts and fruit; reserve. Beat egg whites on high speed of electric mixer until foamy. Add ¼ cup sugar gradually, beating until soft peaks are formed. In another bowl sift together flour, baking powder, salt and sugar; add shortening, milk and flavoring; beat 1 minute at low speed. Add egg whites and beat 2 minutes longer. Fold in Brazil nuts and fruit. Turn into 9×5×3-inch greased loaf pan lined with wax paper. Bake 65 minutes in moderate oven (350°). Cool 15 minutes. Remove from pan. Cool before slicing.

Makes 1 loaf cake.

BRAZIL NUT COFFEE CAKE

1½ cups sifted flour
½ cup sugar
2 teaspoons baking powder
½ teaspoon salt
½ cup milk
2 eggs
1 teaspoon vanilla
¼ cup melted butter
BRAZIL NUT FILLING

Sift together flour, sugar, baking powder and salt. Combine milk, eggs, and vanilla; stir into dry ingredients. Slowly add melted butter. Stir gently only until blended. Pour half of batter into a lightly greased 9-inch pie pan. Sprinkle with Brazil Nut Filling; spread remaining batter over filling. Bake in hot oven (400°) 20 minutes. Cut into wedges; serve hot.

Makes 1 9-inch coffee cake.

BRAZIL NUT FILLING

1 *cup chopped Brazil nuts*
½ *cup brown sugar, firmly packed*
½ *teaspoon nutmeg*
2 *teaspoons cinnamon*
2 *tablespoons melted butter*

Combine and blend ingredients. May be used as filling or crumb topping.

BRAZIL NUT NESSELRODE PIE

2 *envelopes unflavored gelatine*
¼ *cup sugar*
1 *quart bottled non-alcoholic eggnog*
2 *teaspoons rum flavoring*
1 *cup heavy cream, whipped*
⅓ *cup chopped maraschino cherries*
⅓ *cup chopped Brazil nuts*
1 10-*inch* BRAZIL NUT CRUST I

Combine gelatine and sugar in top of double boiler. Stir in 1 cup of the cold eggnog. Place over boiling water and stir until gelatine and sugar are dissolved. Remove from heat; stir in rum flavoring and remaining eggnog. Chill until slightly thicker than the consistency of unbeaten egg white. Whip gelatine mixture until light and fluffy; fold in whipped cream. Fold in maraschino cherries and nuts. Turn into Brazil Nut Crust I; chill until firm. Garnish with additional whipped cream, pieces of maraschino cherry and citron "holly" leaves.

Makes 1 10-inch pie.

BRAZIL NUT CRUST I

1 cup ground Brazil nuts
2 tablespoons sugar

Mix Brazil nuts with sugar in a 9-inch pie plate. Press mixture with the back of a tablespoon against the bottom and sides, up to the rim of the pie plate. If a toasted flavor is desired, bake in hot oven (400°) 8 minutes, or until lightly browned. Cool.

CHOCOLATE CHIFFON PIE I

1 envelope unflavored gelatine
½ cup sugar
¼ teaspoon salt
1 cup milk
2 eggs, separated
1 6-ounce package (1 cup) semi-sweet chocolate morsels
1 teaspoon vanilla
½ cup heavy cream, whipped
1 9-inch BRAZIL NUT CRUST I

Mix together gelatine, ¼ cup sugar and salt in top of double boiler. Stir in milk, egg yolks and semi-sweet chocolate morsels. Place over boiling water and cook, stirring constantly, until gelatine dissolves and chocolate is melted (about 6 minutes). Remove from heat; beat with rotary beater until chocolate is blended. Stir in vanilla. Chill until mixture mounds slightly when dropped from a spoon. Beat egg whites until stiff, but not dry. Gradually add remaining ¼ cup sugar and beat until stiff. Fold into gelatine mixture; fold in whipped cream. Turn into Brazil Nut Crust I; chill until firm. Garnish with additional whipped cream and finely chopped or sliced Brazil nuts, if desired.

Makes 1 9-inch pie.

CHOCOLATE CHIFFON PIE II

1 *envelope unflavored gelatine*
¾ *cup sugar*
⅛ *teaspoon salt*
1 *egg, separated*
¾ *cup milk*
2 *squares (2 ounces) unsweetened chocolate*
1 *cup ice-cold evaporated milk, whipped*
1 *teaspoon vanilla*
1 *9-inch* BRAZIL NUT CRUST II
½ *cup heavy cream, whipped*

Mix gelatine, sugar and salt in top of double boiler. Combine egg yolk and milk and add to gelatine mixture. Add chocolate. Cook over boiling water until chocolate is melted, stirring often. Remove from heat and beat with a rotary beater until smooth. Chill until mixture mounds slightly when dropped from a spoon. Fold in whipped evaporated milk and vanilla. Turn into prepared Brazil Nut Crust II; chill until firm. To serve, spread with whipped cream. If desired, garnish with toasted Brazil-nut slices.

Makes 1 9-inch pie.

NOTE: To whip evaporated milk, chill milk in freezer tray of refrigerator until ice crystals form around edge. Turn into chilled bowl and whip with rotary beater or high speed of electric mixer until milk is of the consistency of whipped cream.

BRAZIL NUT CRUST II

¼ *cup sugar*
⅛ *teaspoon salt*
1½ *cups ground Brazil nuts*
1 *egg white*

Grease 9-inch pie plate with butter or margarine; line bottom with wax paper, then grease paper. Add sugar and salt to ground nuts; mix well. Beat egg white until it holds soft peaks; add to nut mixture; combine thoroughly. Turn mixture into prepared pan and press firmly over bottom and sides. Bake in a moderately hot oven (375°) 12 to 15 minutes, or until lightly browned. Remove from oven and carefully loosen sides of crust from pan with thin-bladed knife. Cool 10 minutes, then lift crust from pan. Remove wax paper; replace crust in plate.

PUMPKIN CHIFFON PIE

1 *envelope unflavored gelatine*
¾ *cup brown sugar, firmly packed*
½ *teaspoon salt*
½ *teaspoon nutmeg*
½ *teaspoon cinnamon*
¼ *teaspoon ginger*
1¼ *cups evaporated milk*
2 *eggs, separated*
1¼ *cups canned or cooked pumpkin*
1 *9-inch* BRAZIL NUT CRUST III

Combine gelatine, ½ cup of the brown sugar, salt and spices in top of double boiler. Stir in evaporated milk, egg yolks and pumpkin. Place over boiling water and cook, stirring occasionally, until gelatine dissolves and mixture is heated through, about 10 minutes. Remove from heat. Cool, stirring occasionally, until mixture is chilled and mounds when dropped from a spoon. Beat egg whites until stiff, but not dry. Gradually add remaining ¼ cup sugar and beat until very stiff. Fold into pumpkin mixture; turn into Brazil Nut Crust III. Chill until firm. If desired, garnish with whipped cream and Brazil-nut curls.

Makes 1 9-inch pie.

BRAZIL NUT CRUST III

¼ cup ground toasted Brazil nuts
Pastry for 1 9-inch single pie crust (packaged or homemade)

Add toasted Brazil nuts to pastry mix or to flour before adding shortening or liquid. Roll out pastry; fit into a 9-inch pie plate. Prick pastry with tines of fork; flute edges. Bake according to package or recipe directions.

ORANGE SUGARED BRAZIL NUTS

1½ cups sugar
1 6-ounce can frozen concentrated orange juice
3 cups whole Brazil nuts

Combine sugar and undiluted concentrate in saucepan; stir until blended. Bring to a boil, stirring constantly. Continue boiling until candy thermometer reaches 236°, or when a small amount of the mixture, when dropped in cold water, forms a soft ball. Remove from heat; add nuts to syrup, stirring constantly. Cool. Stir until mixture begins to thicken and becomes sugary. Drop nuts by teaspoon on wax paper.
Makes 1½ pounds.

BRAZIL NUT FUDGE

¾ cup evaporated milk
1 8-ounce jar marshmallow cream
¼ cup butter or margarine
1½ cups sugar
¼ teaspoon salt
2 6-ounce packages (1 cup each) semi-sweet chocolate morsels
1 teaspoon vanilla
1 cup chopped Brazil nuts

Combine evaporated milk, marshmallow cream, butter, sugar and salt in saucepan. Bring to a full boil, stirring conantly; boil 5 minutes, over moderate heat, stirring constantly. emove from heat and add semi-sweet chocolate morsels and nilla, stirring until smooth. Add nuts. Turn into greased ×8×2-inch square pan. Chill until firm.

Makes about 2 pounds.

BRAZIL NUT BRITTLE

2 cups sugar
¼ teaspoon soda
1½ cups ground Brazil nuts
⅔ cup (4 ounces) semi-sweet chocolate pieces, optional

Put sugar in heavy skillet. Place over low heat and stir nstantly until sugar melts. It is important to keep the mix-re stirred constantly over low heat to get a light, even ramelization of the sugar. Just as soon as all of the sugar has elted, add the soda and stir in 1 cup of the Brazil nuts. Turn to a greased baking sheet and roll out with rolling pin until e brittle is slightly less than ¼ inch thick. Before the candy cool, mark quickly into squares with a sharp knife. If de-ed, brittle may be covered with chocolate. Melt chocolate top of double boiler. When brittle is cold, spread with the elted chocolate and sprinkle with the remaining ½ cup of azil nuts. Break into pieces when chocolate hardens.

Makes about 1¾ pounds.

QUICK BRAZIL NUT CANDY PATTIES

2 cups light brown sugar, firmly packed
½ cup water
1 teaspoon vanilla
¾ cup chopped Brazil nuts

Combine sugar and water in large saucepan; cook over low at, stirring constantly, until mixture boils. Continue cooking, without stirring, until candy thermometer registers 240° or when a small amount dropped in cold water forms a sof[t] ball. Remove from heat; beat until creamy and thickened. Add vanilla and nuts; drop by teaspoonfuls onto aluminum foil.*

Makes about 2½ dozen.

* If mixture become too firm, add a small amount of water and return t[o] heat. Stir until candy melts, then continue as before.

CASHEWS

THE CASHEW

Of all the trees from which we take edible nuts the cashew is the most unusual, as it is the only tree known to bear fruit with an *exterior* seed.

Native to Brazil and the West Indies, the cashew was introduced into India, East Africa, Mozambique and Kenya by early Portuguese explorers, and it is from these sources 13,000 miles away that we in the United States derive our supply—and we consume over 90 per cent of the world's cashew product. The majority of the cashew nuts come from India.

The cashew is a low-growing evergreen bearing flowers which grow in clusters at the ends of its branches. It may grow under adverse conditions where soil is poor and rainfall slight, but it thrives best in the tropics not far from the sea. The cashew flower changes into a bright-colored (orange or yellow) pear-shaped fruit called the "cashew apple," which is eaten in the countries where the tree flourishes. The fermented juice of this apple makes a refreshing drink and a flavoring which is utilized in madeira wine.

Attached to the basal portion of the cashew fruit is the olive-colored, kidney-shaped nut, which ripens two months after flowering and is usually left to fall from the trees before being gathered. The nut is encased in a leathery double shell, between the layers of which is a honeycomb-like membrane containing a powerful oil which may irritate and burn the human skin but which is exceedingly useful in protecting the nut from insects. This oil is driven off when the nut is roasted to make the shells easy to remove, after which the cashew kernels are removed by hand and graded for market.

The cashew is a nut which possesses a rich, meaty sweetness that is very individual. It is a great favorite when eaten plain or in salted mixtures. It is unusual when sautéed in butter and served with beverages, and it adds distinction to any food or confection of which it is a part, for its savor lingers delicately on the taste buds and gives a feeling of real gustatory satisfaction.

CASHEW MEAT BALLS

1½ pounds ground beef
½ pound ground pork
2 eggs
½ cup milk
1 tablespoon mustard seed
2½ teaspoons salt
1 teaspoon pepper
½ teaspoon crushed garlic
½ cup chopped cashews
12 salted soda crackers
¼ pound processed Cheddar cheese
2 cans (20 ounces each) tomatoes
2 cans (8 ounces each) Spanish style tomato sauce
2 small onions, sliced
1 8-ounce package noodles, cooked

Mix together the ground meats, eggs, milk, mustard seed, 2 teaspoons of the salt, ½ teaspoon of the pepper, and garlic. Put the nut meats, crackers, and cheese through the fine blade of the food chopper; mix thoroughly with the meat mixture. Roll into balls about the size of a walnut, and place in a 3-quart casserole. Combine the tomatoes, tomato sauce, onions, the remaining ½ teaspoon salt and ½ teaspoon pepper, and pour over meat balls. Cover and bake in a moderate oven (350°) 1 hour. Serve over hot noodles.

Makes 6 servings.

CASHEW SOUR-MILK WAFFLES

2 cups sifted cake flour
1½ teaspoons double-acting baking powder
¼ teaspoon soda
¼ teaspoon salt
1 tablespoon sugar
½ cup chopped cashews
2 egg yolks, well beaten
1¼ cups sour milk or buttermilk
4 tablespoons melted butter or margarine
2 egg whites, stiffly beaten

Sift flour once, measure, add baking powder, soda, salt, and sugar, and sift again. Add nuts and mix. Combine egg yolks, milk, and butter; add to flour mixture, beating until smooth. Fold in egg whites. Bake in hot waffle iron. Serve with maple blended syrup and butter.

Makes 4 or 5 4-section waffles.

CASHEW MUFFINS

2 cups sifted flour
2 teaspoons double-acting baking powder
2 tablespoons sugar
¼ teaspoon salt
½ cup chopped cashews
1 egg, well beaten
1 cup milk
4 tablespoons melted butter or other shortening

Sift flour once, measure, add baking powder, sugar, and salt, and sift again. Add nuts and mix. Combine egg, milk, and shortening; add to flour mixture, beating only enough to dampen all flour. Bake in greased muffin pans in hot oven (425°) 25 minutes or until done.

Makes 24 small muffins.

CASHEW NUT BUTTER COOKIES

½ cup butter
1 cup sugar
1 egg
1 teaspoon grated orange rind
2 tablespoons orange juice
1 cup ground cashews
2 cups sifted flour
2 teaspoons baking powder
½ teaspoon salt
¼ teaspoon rum flavoring

Cream butter; gradually add sugar and beat until light and fluffy. Stir in egg, orange rind, orange juice and cashews. Sift together flour, baking powder and salt. Add to creamed mixture; mix well. Stir in rum flavoring. Put through cooky press onto an ungreased baking sheet. Bake in moderately hot oven (375°) 8 to 10 minutes.

Makes approximately 5 dozen cookies.

CASHEW NUGGET COOKIES

½ cup butter
1 cup sifted confectioners' sugar
1 egg
1½ cups sifted flour
¼ teaspoon salt
½ cup finely chopped cashews
¼ teaspoon vanilla
Red jam
Cashew halves

Cream butter, sugar and egg together. Sift flour with salt, and add to creamed mixture with finely chopped cashews and vanilla. Chill dough until firm. Roll pieces of dough into balls. With finger tip, make depression in top of each ball. Bake in moderate oven (350°) 15 minutes. While warm, fill centers with jam and top with cashew halves.

Makes 3½ dozen cookies.

CASHEW DROP COOKIES

1 cup sifted flour
1 teaspoon double-acting baking powder
¼ teaspoon salt
6 tablespoons butter or other shortening
½ cup sugar
1 egg, well beaten
1 cup chopped cashews
1 teaspoon vanilla
¼ cup milk

Sift flour once, measure, add baking powder and salt, and sift again. Cream butter thoroughly and add sugar gradually, creaming well; then add egg, ½ cup of the nuts, and vanilla and beat thoroughly. Add flour alternately with milk, mixing well after each addition. Drop from teaspoon on greased baking sheet. Sprinkle with remaining ½ cup nuts. Bake in hot oven (425°) 8 to 10 minutes, or until done.

Makes 2 dozen.

CASHEW ICEBOX COOKIES

4 cups sifted flour
3 teaspoons double-acting baking powder
¼ teaspoon salt
1 cup butter or other shortening
2 cups sugar
½ cup brown sugar, firmly packed
2 eggs, well beaten
1 cup chopped cashews
1 tablespoon vanilla

Sift flour once, measure, add baking powder and salt and sift again. Cream butter and add sugars gradually, creaming thoroughly; add eggs, nuts, and vanilla and beat well. Add flour gradually, mixing well after each addition. Shape into rolls 1½ inches in diameter and roll in waxed paper. Chill overnight, or until firm enough to slice. Cut in ⅛-inch slices; bake on ungreased baking sheet in hot oven (425°) 5 minutes, or until done.

Makes about 7 dozen cookies.

BITTERSWEET CASHEW CLUSTERS

4 squares candy-making chocolate cut in pieces
2 squares unsweetened chocolate
2 cups cashews

Melt chocolate over hot water. Add nuts, stirring until well mixed. Drop from teaspoon on wax paper and let stand until firm.

Makes 2 dozen.

CASHEW MERINGUES

1 egg white
½ cup sugar
½ cup broken cashews
¼ teaspoon vanilla

Beat egg white until foamy throughout. Add sugar gradually, beating after each addition until sugar is blended. Then continue beating until mixture will stand in peaks. Fold in nuts and vanilla. Drop from teaspoon on greased foil-lined baking sheet. Bake in moderate oven (350°) 10 to 12 minutes, or until delicately browned.

Makes 2 dozen meringues.

CASHEW CUPCAKES

1⅔ cups sifted cake flour
1½ teaspoons double-acting baking powder
⅓ cup butter or other shortening
1 cup sugar
2 eggs, unbeaten
1 cup chopped cashews
½ cup milk
1 teaspoon lemon extract or vanilla
2 tablespoons melted butter
¼ cup light brown sugar, firmly packed

Sift flour once, measure, add baking powder, and sift together three times. Cream butter thoroughly, add sugar gradually, and cream together until light and fluffy. Add eggs, one at a time, beating well after each. Add ½ cup of the chopped nuts and mix. Add flour mixture alternately with milk, a small amount at a time, beating after each addition until smooth. Add flavoring. Turn into greased cupcake pans, filling them ⅔ full. Bake in moderately hot oven (375°) 15 minutes. Before removing from oven, combine melted butter and sugar, add remaining ½ cup chopped nuts and mix; sprinkle mixture on top of cakes and bake 5 minutes longer, or until cakes are done.

Makes 2 dozen small cupcakes.

CASHEW WHIMSIES

1 egg white
½ cup light brown sugar, firmly packed
1 cup broken cashews
½ teaspoon vanilla

Beat egg white until foamy. Add sugar gradually, beating after each addition until sugar is blended. Then continue beating until mixture will stand in peaks. Fold in nuts and vanilla. Drop from teaspoon on greased foil-lined baking sheet. Bake in moderate oven (350°) 10 to 15 minutes, or until delicately browned.

Makes 2 dozen pieces.

CASHEW NUT ROLL

¼ teaspoon double-acting baking powder
⅛ teaspoon salt
2 eggs unbeaten
6 tablespoons sifted sugar
6 tablespoons sifted cake flour
½ teaspoon vanilla

Combine baking powder, salt, and eggs in bowl. Place over smaller bowl of hot water and beat with rotary egg beater, adding sugar gradually until mixture becomes thick and light-colored. Remove bowl from hot water. Fold in flour and vanilla. Turn into 13×9-inch pan which as been greased, lined with wax paper to within ½ inch of edge, and again greased. Bake in hot oven (400°) 13 minutes. Quickly cut off crisp edges of cake. Invert on cloth covered with confectioners' sugar; remove wax paper. Spread with Cashew Nut Filling and roll. Wrap roll in cloth and let stand on rack until cool.

CASHEW NUT FILLING

1 cup chopped cashews
3 tablespoons butter
3 tablespoons milk
1 cup sifted confectioners' sugar
½ teaspoon vanilla

Cook nuts slowly in butter until well toasted, stirring constantly. Remove from heat and add milk. Add sugar gradually, beating until smooth; add vanilla. Cool until thick enough to spread.

CASHEW NUT BRITTLE

2 cups sugar
½ cup light corn syrup
½ cup water
2 tablespoons butter
½ teaspoon salt
⅛ teaspoon soda
1½ cups coarsely broken cashews

Combine sugar, corn syrup, and water in saucepan. Place over low heat and stir constantly until sugar is dissolved. Continue cooking, without stirring, until a small amount of syrup forms a hard ball in cold water (270°). Add butter and salt and continue cooking, stirring frequently, until a small amount of syrup becomes brittle in cold water (300°). Remove from heat. Add soda and nuts, stirring only enough to mix. Pour in thin sheet on slightly greased surface. Do not scrape mixture from sides of saucepan. Let cool 30 seconds, hen lift edges of brittle and stretch to as thin a sheet as possible. Mark into squares while warm, or break into pieces when cold.

Makes 80 2-inch squares.

CASHEW NUT JUMBLES

¾ cup unsulphured molasses
6 tablespoons sugar
¼ cup butter
⅛ teaspoon soda
1 teaspoon vanilla
1 teaspoon lemon extract
½ cup dates, finely chopped
1 cup raisins
2 cups chopped cashews

Combine molasses and sugar in large saucepan; cook over low heat, stirring constantly, until mixture boils. Continue cooking without stirring until candy thermometer registers 260°, or when a small amount dropped in cold water becomes slightly brittle. Add butter; continue to cook to 280°, or when a small amount dropped in cold water becomes brittle. Remove from heat; add soda and stir. Add flavorings, dates, raisins and cashews. Cool about 1 minute. Quickly roll into bite-size balls. When cold, wrap in wax paper or aluminum foil.

Makes about 1½ pounds.

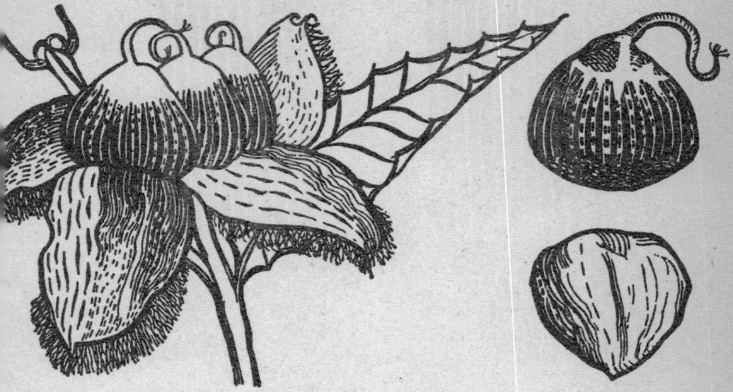

CHESTNUTS

THE CHESTNUT

Have you traveled through the forest lands of America, wondering and noticing the great expanses of tall dead tree trunks? They are the great "ghosts"—a testament to the grandeur of the once proud American chestnut. If you have felt a sense of loss and tragedy it has been well founded, for this stalwart, known as a rich source of food for animals and humans alike in every nation in which it flourishes, has fallen prey here in America to a dread fungus disease which has ravaged our riches and laid bare our lands on every side.

The history of the chestnut leads us to believe that its origin lies in Asia Minor, Armenia, the Caucasus and North Africa, where it has been cultivated from time immemorial. It was introduced to Europe by the Greeks; its present name comes to us from the Roman *castanea*, from Castanus, a town of Magnesia, where it grew in great profusion and was popular for its beautiful foliage and nourishing nut. Carried to Britain by the Romans, these glorious trees have been known to reach a height of 100 feet and an age of over 1000 years.

In the past they have served as a source of old-fashioned medicinal remedies such as: a *tincture of leaves* used externally for chilblains, irritating eczemas, rheumatic or neuralgic pains; an *infusion of the bark* taken three or four times daily, successful for intermittent fevers and for easing the pain of uclers; *chestnut powder* made from the finely ground insides, taken two times daily to relieve colic and intestinal disorders;

and the *essence*, made from boiling the chestnuts in water, that was added to the bath to soothe those suffering from skin troubles.

For almost 2000 years the chestnut has been an important article of food throughout Southern Europe, and in some of the mountainous districts it is almost the "staff of life." It is eaten raw and enjoyed roasted, stewed, dried and ground into a flour from which a coarse cake or bread is made. The chestnut is rich in nutritional values and highly important in the diets of the Spanish and Portuguese. In Italy and France recipes using the chestnut in puddings, desserts, main dishes, breads, etc., have been devised, and chestnut meal has long been used in Germany to make a delicious bread which is served with coffee. The sacred significance of the chestnut is evident in its solemn use as a sweetmeat on St. Simon's Day and in its distribution to the poor on the feast of St. Martin.

Chestnuts we eat here in America are either imported or come from trees of the European species that have been grown in the United States. It is quite probable that we are indebted to the family of Dupont de Nemours, who left France sometime before the Revolution to settle in Delaware where they engaged principally in the manufacture of gunpowder and collaterally in the growth of the chestnut. It is known that they were the first to raise the European chestnut to a bearing size in this country, and it is entirely possible that *all* of the hardy trees of this species now scattered about the country are the direct descendants of that old Dupont stock.

Serious efforts are being made to create a hybrid of American and European chestnut trees which can resist the dread fungus disease, and some California nurserymen have taken to the cultivation of chestnuts from a species of Japanese tree with good results. Nevertheless in this country, where we have an abundance of other cereal foods, we have tended to relegate the chestnut—which once, bursting from its burr, was a joy to the sight of every American boy and girl—to the role of an ingredient in the stuffing of our holiday birds.

Perhaps in time we shall see once more the stately chestnut with its long, feathery blossoms and handsome foliage spreading forty to fifty feet replacing, along our lawns and in our forests, the "ghost trees" which remind us too sadly of the lost richness of beauty and nutrition which once covered our land. Until then we can enjoy the flavor and gustatory delight of this nut in the dishes which come steaming from the kitchen of a creative cook.

SWISS CHESTNUT CREAM SOUP

3 cups parboiled chestnuts
2 cups water
¾ teaspoon salt
1 teaspoon sugar
1½ teaspoons thinly sliced lemon peel
2 cups milk
4 cups chicken stock
Salt
¼ teaspoon pepper
2 tablespoons cornstarch
1 tablespoon butter
⅛ teaspoon paprika
Whipped cream

Boil chestnuts in water for ½ hour or until tender with ¾ teaspoon salt, sugar and lemon peel. Press through sieve, add milk, chicken stock, salt to taste, and pepper. Simmer for 15 minutes more. Add cornstarch dissolved in 1 tablespoon of water. Heat until mixture boils. Add butter and stir until melted. Sprinkle with paprika. Top with whipped cream. *Makes 8 to 10 servings.*

CHESTNUT SHERRY BISQUE

4 cups boiled chestnuts
3 tablespoons butter, melted
2 tablespoons flour
1 teaspoon Worcestershire sauce
½ teaspoon dry mustard
1 teaspoon salt
⅛ teaspoon paprika
⅛ teaspoon soda
2½ cups milk
½ cup heavy cream
¼ cup sherry
Whipped cream

Mash chestnuts or force through a sieve. Reserve. Blend butter, flour, Worcestershire sauce, mustard, salt, paprika and soda. Add milk and cream slowly. Cook over moderate heat 5 minutes or until slightly thickened. Stir constantly. Add chestnuts and sherry, heat to serving temperature. Top with whipped cream.

Makes 6 servings.

CHESTNUT AND MUSHROOM CASSEROLE

- 4 *cups cooked chestnuts*
- 1½ *pounds mushrooms*
- 3 *tablespoons butter or margarine*
- 1 *egg*
- ¼ *teaspoon dry mustard*
- 1 *teaspoon Worcestershire sauce*
- ¼ *teaspoon sugar*
- ½ *teaspoon salt*
- ⅛ *teaspoon pepper*
- ¼ *cup sherry*
- 1 *cup light cream*
- ½ *cup coarse buttered crumbs*

Cut chestnuts in half if large; use them whole if small. Slice mushrooms, sauté in butter or margarine 5 minutes. Add chestnuts, mixing well. Combine egg and seasonings, beating egg to a froth. Add sherry slowly, beating constantly, then add cream. Mix with hot mushrooms, turn into greased baking dish: sprinkle with crumbs and bake in hot oven (425°) 10 minutes.

Makes 4 to 6 servings.

CHESTNUT DRESSING

- 3 *cups soft bread crumbs*
- ¼ *cup melted butter or margarine*
- 1 *teaspoon salt*
- ½ *teaspoon pepper*
- 3 *tablespoons chopped parsley*
- ½ *cup milk*
- 2 *cups chopped cooked chestnuts*

Mix bread, melted butter, salt, pepper and parsley. Add milk and chestnuts. Use to stuff poultry or duck.

Makes 3 cups.

HOLIDAY CHESTNUT PUREE

6 cups cooked chestnuts
½ cup chopped ginger, preserved in syrup
⅓ cup melted butter or margarine
3 tablespoons light cream
½ teaspoon salt
2 tablespoons rum

Rub hot chestnuts through a sieve, add ginger, ¼ cup of the melted butter or margarine, cream and salt and beat well. Turn into shallow baking dish. Mix remaining butter or margarine with 2 tablespoons syrup drained from ginger, pour over chestnut purée and put under low broiler heat until glazed. Pour rum over surface of pudding and light just before serving. Serve as a vegetable or as a dessert with sweetened cream, whipped.

Makes 6 servings.

PUREE DE MARRONS

1½ pounds chestnuts (4 cups mashed)
¼ teaspoon mace
Dash red pepper
⅛ teaspoon curry powder
⅔ cup light cream

Peel chestnuts and simmer until soft. Drain, mash and add seasonings. Stir well and add enough cream to moisten. Place in buttered baking dish and brown under broiler. If desired, a beaten egg white can be piled on top of chestnut mixture. Then bake in slow oven (325°) for 15 minutes or until egg white is golden brown.

Makes 6 servings.

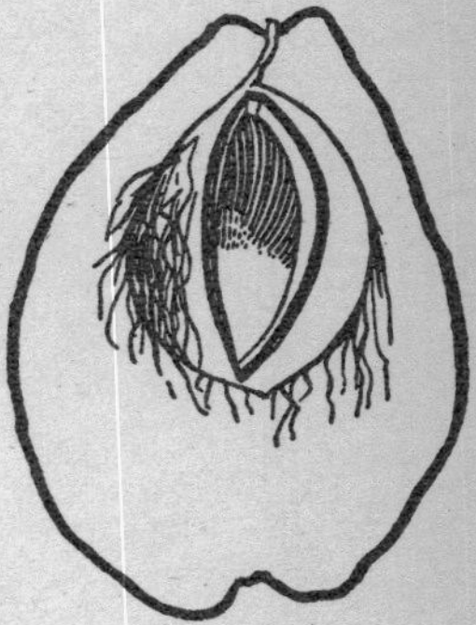

COCONUTS

COCONUT

The coconut is the largest and one of the most widely known of edible nuts. It is probably utilized in more ways for a greater variety of purposes than any other nut known to man.

The lofty palm tree grows along the shores bordering tropical islands whence it has been self-propelled, since it can float on water. It is widely cultivated for commercial purposes.

The name coconut comes from the Portuguese word for monkey, *macaco*, since the nut with its three "eyes" suggests the face of that little animal. From one of these "eyes" of the nut the young tree sprouts, and from the other two "eyes" the roots of the new palm form and grow.

Coconuts provide the main items of food and drink for millions of people living in lands where this beautiful 60–100-foot tree grows. The trees begin to bear 75 to 200 nuts annually around the sixth or seventh year of life and may continue to bear from sixty to eighty years.

While many nuts drop spontaneously from the trees, others are gathered by agile workers who climb the straight trunks by means of slings or by notches cut like steps in the trunk.

Introduction to some of the uses to which the coconut is put provides an insight into why it is considered the complete "staff of life" in countries where it is plentiful and why it has been called the most useful tree in existence.

The fruit, eaten raw or cooked, is a substitute for meat and bread; the terminal buds and inner part of the young stems are considered vegetable delicacies; the liquid milk of the young nut is a nutritious drink, and the fermented liquid extracted from the flower buds is called "toddy" and taken as a drink; when further distilled this liquid produces a brandy-like beverage called "arrack"; when this liquid is boiled down, a sugar called "jaggery" is produced. The leaves of the coconut palm may be interwoven as roofing and thatching material; baskets, fans, brooms, fencing, and mats are made from the midribs of the leaves. The "coir," which is the coarse fibers growing in the husk, is used for the making of ropes, cables, cordage, matting, brushes and as a substitute for horsehair in the stuffing of furniture and bedding. Some of the shells of the coconut are used as fuel, since they give off intense heat, while others are saved for the making of carved and ornamented containers of all kinds. Very occasionally a small concretion of "coconut pearl" may be found in the cavity of a coconut, blue-white in color, lustrous and harder in texture than a true pearl, this "jewel," the size of a cherry, is much prized and has often been set to be worn like a costly gem.

If left unopened when ripe, the coconut becomes rancid. In order to avoid this, the nuts are opened promptly and the meat is dried to create a product known as copra. Copra's greatest commercial value lies in its coconut oil and the products which are made from it, but of course the commodity best known and used in large quantity by the cuisinières of the world in the making of cakes, candies and desserts is shredded or desiccated coconut. This product alone has made the coconut so desirable that we must remind ourselves of the other attributes.

Even in our modern day it is interesting to remember the truth of the ancient Syrian saying:

> *"If a man were placed on earth with nothing else but the coconut tree, he could live in happiness and contentment."*

COCONUT BAKED TUNA

2 pimientos
1 10½-ounce can condensed cream of mushroom soup
¼ cup milk
1 6½-ounce can chunk-style tuna, drained
2 cups cooked rice
¼ teaspoon Worcestershire sauce
Few grains pepper
½ cup grated coconut
¼ cup sliced toasted filberts

Dice one pimiento and mix with soup, milk, flaked tuna, rice, seasonings, and coconut. Pour into 1-quart casserole and garnish with strips of pimiento and sliced filberts. Bake in a moderate oven (350°) 30 minutes.

Makes 6 servings.

EAST INDIA SALAD

½ cup yogurt
2 tablespoons mayonnaise
¼ teaspoon grated orange rind
½ teaspoon salt
⅛ teaspoon curry powder
1 large orange
2 cups diced cooked turkey or chicken
1 cup sliced celery
½ cup flaked coconut
½ cup blanched slivered almonds

Combine yogurt, mayonnaise, orange rind, salt and curry powder; chill. Peel, section and dice orange into a large bowl; toss lightly with yogurt mixture and remaining ingredients. Chill before serving.

Makes 4 to 6 servings.

HONEY CRUNCHIES

⅔ cup honey
2 tablespoons butter or margarine
¼ cup evaporated milk
¼ teaspoon salt
½ teaspoon vanilla
2 cups cornflakes
½ cup whole bran
1 cup fine-grated coconut

Combine honey, butter, evaporated milk, salt, and vanilla in a large saucepan. Bring to a boil over medium heat, stirring. Boil and stir for 3 minutes. Remove from heat. Add cornflakes, whole bran and coconut. Using 2 teaspoons, drop mounds of mixture on aluminum foil- or wax paper-lined baking sheets. When cool, keep in refrigerator.

Makes about 2 dozen.

COCONUT SCOTCH COOKIES

¾ cup shortening
1 cup brown sugar, firmly packed
1 egg
¼ cup milk
½ teaspoon vanilla
2¼ cups sifted flour
1 teaspoon soda
½ teaspoon salt
1 cup chopped nuts
1 cup flaked coconut
½ cup butterscotch chips

Cream shortening, sugar, and egg together until fluffy. Add milk and vanilla; mix well. Sift flour with soda and salt. Add to creamed ingredients and mix well. Fold in nuts, coconut, and butterscotch chips. Drop by teaspoonfuls onto greased cooky sheet. Bake in a hot oven (400°) 10–12 minutes.

Makes 5½ dozen.

COCONUT CRISPIES

2½ cups sifted flour
½ teaspoon soda
½ teaspoon salt
1 cup butter or margarine
2½ cups brown sugar, firmly packed
2 eggs
2 squares melted unsweetened chocolate
½ cup finely chopped macadamia nuts
½ cup grated coconut
Macadamia nuts in large pieces for topping

Sift the flour, soda and salt together. Cream butter and add sugar gradually. Cream well. Add eggs one at a time, beating well after each addition. Add the melted chocolate. Then add dry ingredients and chopped macadamia nuts. Add grated coconut and blend well. Drop this mixture from a teaspoon onto greased baking sheets. Place the larger pieces of macadamia nuts on top of each Crispie. Bake in moderate oven (350°) 8 to 10 minutes.

Makes about 7 dozen Crispies.

MACADAMIA MACAROONS

1 cup butter
1 cup sugar
1 cup brown sugar, firmly packed
2 large eggs
1 teaspoon vanilla
2 cups sifted flour
1 teaspoon baking powder
1 teaspoon soda
1 teaspoon salt
2 cups cornflakes
2 cups quick-cooking rolled oats
1 cup shredded coconut
1 cup chopped macadamia nuts

Cream the butter and add sugars gradually. Cream well. Add the eggs one at a time and beat well after each addition. Add vanilla. Sift the flour, baking powder, soda and salt together. Add cornflakes, rolled oats, coconut and macadamia nuts. Combine and add to creamed mixture. Blend well. Form into small balls by hand. Place on greased baking sheets and bake in a moderately hot oven (375°) 12 to 14 minutes.

Makes about 9 dozen.

COCONUT SNAPS

2¼ cups sifted flour
1 teaspoon soda
⅛ teaspoon salt
¾ cup brown sugar
¾ cup sugar
¾ cup brown sugar, firmly packed
1 egg
1 teaspoon vanilla
1 cup flaked coconut
1 cup macadamia nuts, coarsely chopped
Candied pineapple pieces

Sift the flour, soda and salt together. Cream butter, then add sugars gradually. Cream well. Add the egg and vanilla and beat well. Turn mixer to low speed and add sifted dry ingredients, coconut and macadamia nuts. Form this mixture into balls the size of a small walnut. Top with a piece of candied pineapple. Place on a greased baking sheet. Bake in a moderately hot oven (375°) about 12 minutes.

Makes about 8 dozen.

VANILLA COCONUT CREAM CAKE

3 eggs
1 cup sugar
3 tablespoons cold water
1½ teaspoons vanilla
1 cup sifted cake flour
1 teaspoon double-acting baking powder
⅛ teaspoon salt
VANILLA COCONUT CREAM

Beat eggs until light and lemon-colored. Gradually add sugar and beat until the mixture is thick and pale. Blend in water and vanilla. Sift flour with baking powder and salt 3 times. Stir into the mixture. Pour batter into an ungreased 9-inch springform pan. Bake in a moderate oven (350°) 40 minutes or until a cake tester inserted in center comes out clean. Cool cake in pan. Top with Vanilla Coconut Cream.

Makes 1 9-inch cake.

VANILLA COCONUT CREAM

- 2 *envelopes unflavored gelatine*
- ½ *cup cold water*
- 2 *cups milk*
- ¾ *cup sugar*
- 2 *egg yolks, beaten*
- 1½ *teaspoons vanilla*
- 1 *cup heavy cream, whipped*
- ⅓ *cup grated coconut*
- *Tinted coconut for garnish*

Soften gelatine in cold water in top of double boiler. Add milk and mix well. Stir in sugar. Place over boiling water and cook, stirring constantly, until gelatine and sugar are dissolved. Pour small amount over beaten egg yolks, stirring constantly. Return to double boiler and cook until mixture is slightly thickened. Remove from double boiler and blend in vanilla. Chill until mixture begins to thicken. Fold in whipped cream and grated coconut and pour over cake. Refrigerate until set. When ready to serve, release spring and remove sides of pan. Sprinkle with tinted coconut.

COCONUT DATE PIE

- 3 *eggs*
- 1 *cup evaporated milk*
- 1 *cup honey*
- 1 *tablespoon lemon juice*
- ½ *teaspoon salt*
- 1 *teaspoon cinnamon*
- ½ *teaspoon nutmeg*
- ¼ *cup fine bread or cracker crumbs*
- 2 *cups fresh dates, chopped*
- 1 *cup fine-grated coconut*
- 1 *unbaked 9-inch pie shell*

Beat eggs slightly. With the exception of the coconut, combine ingredients in order given, pour into pie shell. Bake in hot oven (425°) 15 minutes. Reduce oven temperature to 325°, sprinkle coconut over top of pie filling and continue to bake for 25 to 30 minutes or until mixture is firm in center.

Makes 6 servings.

COCONUT TRIO BARS

FIRST LAYER

¼ cup butter
1 cup sifted flour
¼ teaspoon salt

Cream butter; add sifted flour and salt and mix until thoroughly blended. Turn into a 9-inch square pan, spread evenly over the bottom and press down with a spatula. Bake in a moderately hot oven (375°) 15 minutes.

SECOND LAYER

2 eggs, well beaten
¾ cup brown sugar, firmly packed
1 cup finely chopped Brazil nuts
¼ teaspoon salt
½ cup shredded coconut
1 teaspoon vanilla
2 tablespoons flour

To well-beaten eggs, add sugar and blend well. Mix in Brazil nuts, coconut and vanilla. Add remaining ingredients. Mix well. Spread evenly over baked first layer. Bake in moderately hot oven (375°) 15 minutes. Remove from oven and cool in pan.

CHOCOLATE FROSTING

1 package (1 cup) semi-sweet chocolate morsels
¼ cup light corn syrup
1 tablespoon water

Melt semi-sweet chocolate morsels over hot, not boiling, water. Stir in light corn syrup and water; mix well. Spread evenly over baked, cooled cooky mixture; sprinkle with chopped nuts. Let stand 30 minutes. Cut in 3×1-inch bars.

Makes 36 bars.

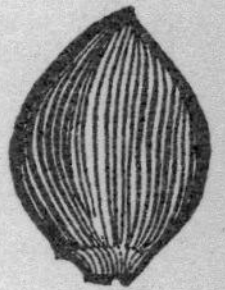

FILBERTS OR HAZELNUTS

THE FILBERT OR HAZELNUT

The small true nut called the filbert is truly the direct descendant of the beaked hazelnut found in almost every woodland. In its cultivated state it exists actually as the selected or improvised form of the wild hazel, a fruit with two bracts which unite to enclose the nut at the base of a long tubular "beak." When the hazel and filbert nuts are ripe and fallen from their husks, there is nothing left to distinguish them one from the other.

The wild hazelnut has been a favorite since early times. Those reserved for planting must be buried in rodentproof boxes in which they are stratified amongst layers of moist sand. The boxes are covered with hardware cloth and heaped with sawdust to prevent frost damage. Generally the nuts germinate in spring before the ground is ready (unless it has been prepared the previous autumn). Cultivators wage a constant battle with birds and animals who will dig up and eat every sprouted nut they can find. Only when the first true leaves have formed on the young trees does the battle seem to subside.

Filberts must be gathered daily as they fall if they are to be enjoyed by any but the wildlife. They can be kept in a warm dry place for many months until needed, and kernels can be refrigerated in a closed jar or a plastic bag.

The fruits we cultivate today are derived from many varieties of trees brought from Europe to the eastern states by early settlers, who attributed occult powers to the forked twig of the hazel. Its branches were used in attempts to divine hidden treasures, veins of metals, and subterranean streams of water. Even criminals were thought to be discovered by its magic powers.

Today of course these uses have been put aside, and the pretty purple filbert acclaimed by Virgil as being "more honored than the vine, the myrtle or even the bay itself" decorates our walks, handsome shrub that it is, while the great orchards of Washington and Oregon yield up the high-quality nuts which find their way to our tables plain, in salads, main dishes, desserts and confections.

FILBERT SOUP

3 tablespoons melted butter
1 cup diced celery
1 cup diced onions
4 tablespoons flour
1 teaspoon salt
¾ teaspoon Worcestershire sauce
⅛ teaspoon pepper
2 cups milk
2 cups chicken bouillon
½ cup ground filberts
½ cup chopped filberts

Melt butter in skillet. Add celery and onions. Sauté until soft. Stir in flour, salt, Worcestershire sauce and pepper. Slowly stir in milk, bouillon and ground filberts. Stir until blended. Simmer for 15 minutes. Serve hot. Garnish with chopped filberts.

Makes 4 to 6 servings.

FILBERT-STUFFED FISH FILLETS

⅓ cup chopped toasted filberts
2 cups cubed bread
1 teaspoon salt
⅛ teaspoon ground black pepper
⅛ teaspoon ground thyme
2 tablespoons chopped onions
¼ cup chopped celery
3 tablespoons butter
1 pound fish fillets
¼ cup catchup
¼ cup water

Combine filberts, bread cubes, ½ teaspoon of the salt, pepper and thyme. Sauté onions and celery in 2 tablespoons of the butter; toss with bread mixture. Arrange half of the fillets in bottom of shallow baking dish; sprinkle with ¼ teaspoon of the salt; top with stuffing mixture. Arrange remaining fillets on top; sprinkle with remaining ¼ teaspoon salt; dot with remaining 1 tablespoon butter. Combine catchup and water; pour over all. Bake in a moderate oven (350°) 30 minutes, until fish is done.

Makes 4 servings.

FILBERT POTATO SCALLOP

¾ cup chopped filberts
3 diced raw potatoes
1 cup grated Cheddar cheese
2 tablespoons finely chopped onions
2 tablespoons butter
½ can condensed cream of mushroom soup
¾ cup milk
1 teaspoon salt
⅛ teaspoon ground black pepper

Arrange alternate layers of filberts, potatoes, cheese and onions in casserole dish. Dot top with butter. Combine soup, milk, salt and pepper; pour over layers in casserole. Bake in a moderate oven (350°) 40 minutes, until potatoes are done.

Makes 4 to 6 servings.

DIPPLES–GREEK PASTRIES

3 eggs
2 cups sifted flour
1 cup honey
¼ cup water
1 cup toasted chopped filberts

Beat eggs; add enough of the flour to make a stiff, workable dough. Knead dough until smooth, shiny and elastic, adding flour as necessary to prevent dough from sticking. Stretch it and roll out to ⅛-inch thickness. Cut strips 2½×1½ inches. Fry in hot fat (375°) until golden brown and puffy. Drain and cool. Combine honey and water, cook over moderate heat to 344°. Cool syrup to 110°. Sprinkle cooled honey mixture over pastries; sprinkle with chopped filberts. Turn pastries over and coat the other side in the same manner.

Makes about 72 medium dipples.

FILBERT CHRISTMAS CAKE

1 cup filberts
2 cups sifted flour
½ teaspoon salt
1 cup butter or shortening
1 cup sugar
4 eggs
1 teaspoon vanilla or brandy flavoring
1 pound mixed candied fruits
¼ pound golden raisins
¼ pound pitted dates, chopped

Toast filberts and chop coarsely. Sift flour; measure. Add salt and sift again. Set aside until ready to use. Cream butter and sugar until light and fluffy. Add eggs one at a time, beating well after each addition. Add flavoring. Combine mixed fruits, raisins and nuts and sprinkle about ¾ cup of the flour over them. Add remaining flour to cake mixture and mix well. Then stir in the floured fruit. Line greased baking pan with wax paper and grease well. Fill pan about ¾ full and bake in a slow oven (300°) about 2 hours or until cake tests done. Store in an airtight container.

Makes about 3 pounds of cake.

FILBERT CHRISTMAS TREE

1 package hot-roll mix
½ cup chopped toasted filberts
¼ cup butter
½ cup brown sugar, firmly packed
2 tablespoons chopped candied cherries
1 tablespoon hot water
1 cup sifted confectioners' sugar
¼ teaspoon vanilla
¼ cup toasted filbert halves
Silver dragees
Candied cherry halves

Prepare hot-roll mix according to package directions. When ready to shape, proceed as follows:

Pat dough into 11-inch square; cut in two diagonally. Each triangle forms half of the tree, with excess dough for base. Fold one 11-inch side of each triangle over to longest side of triangle. Trim off uncovered dough to make edges even. Reserve for shaping trunk. Unfold each triangle. Combine chopped filberts, butter, brown sugar and candied cherries. Spread filling on half of each triangle; save a little for trunk. Fold uncovered half of triangle over filling. Place folded edges of each triangle together to form tree shape. With scissors, slash top layer of dough on each side every inch from bottom to top of tree to form branches. Roll reserved dough into small rectangle. Spread with filling; roll. Place at bottom of tree to form trunk. Let rise in warm place until doubled in bulk, about 45 minutes. Bake on greased baking sheet in a moderately hot oven (375°) 25–30 minutes. Combine hot water, powdered sugar and vanilla for glaze. Spread on tree while warm. Decorate with filbert halves, silver dragees and cherry halves.

Makes 8–10 servings.

QUICK FRUITCAKE DESSERT

¾ cup cut dates
¾ cup candied fruits
3 cups tiny marshmallows
¾ cup chopped toasted filberts
¾ cup cream
2 tablespoons brandy or rum, if desired
2 cups vanilla wafer crumbs

Combine dates, fruits, marshmallows, nuts, cream and brandy; mix well. Add half of the crumbs, mix well, then work in remainder of crumbs. Pack into small loaf pan 7⅝× 3¾ inches. Cover; refrigerate 24 hours. To serve, cut in slices and garnish with whipped cream.

Makes 8 servings.

FILBERT SURPRISE BALLS

(No-Cooking Candy)

1½ cups toasted filberts
3 tablespoons butter
3 squares unsweetened chocolate, grated
1¼ cups sifted confectioners' sugar

Reserve ½ cup filberts (36 whole nuts). Grind or chop fine the remaining nuts. Combine butter and grated chocolate stir in finely chopped nuts and confectioners' sugar. Blend. Form into balls with a whole filbert in the center. Roll each ball in additional ground filberts or confectioners' sugar and chill.

Makes about 36 candies.

HAZELNUT STUFFING FOR DUCK

½ cup chopped hazelnuts
¼ cup chopped celery
2 tablespoons chopped onions
¼ cup melted butter
1 quart day-old bread cubes or crumbs
1 orange, sections and juice
¾ teaspoon salt
Few grains pepper
¼ teaspoon sage, or poultry seasoning
¼ cup raisins
¼ cup stock or bouillon

Sauté nuts, celery, and onions in butter. Combine with soft bread crumbs, orange sections and juice, seasonings, raisins and stock. Mix well; stuff duck.

Makes enough for 1 5-pound duck.

HAZELNUT STUFFING FOR FISH

4 strips bacon
2 tablespoons chopped onions
2 tablespoons chopped parsley
1 tablespoon lemon juice
½ teaspoon celery salt
⅛ teaspoon pepper
½ teaspoon savory
½ cup chopped hazelnuts
2 cups small bread cubes

Cook bacon until crisp. Drain on absorbent paper. Add chopped onions to bacon fat and sauté until golden brown. Remove from heat and stir in parsley, lemon juice, celery salt, pepper and savory. Break bacon into small pieces; add with chopped hazelnuts to bread. Pour onion mixture with bacon fat over dry ingredients and toss well.

To stuff fish, wash well and pat dry. Salt cavity lightly; fill with stuffing. Skewer opening. Brush fish with melted butter or shortening. Place in greased roasting pan and bake in a hot oven (400°), allowing 10 minutes for each pound of fish Garnish with lemon slices and parsley.

Makes enough for 3–4-pound fish.

CRISP HAZELNUT DROPS

- *¾ cup brown sugar, firmly packed*
- *½ cup butter or shortening*
- *1 egg*
- *1 teaspoon vanilla*
- *1 cup sifted flour*
- *2 teaspoons baking powder*
- *½ teaspoon salt*
- *1½ cups sugar-coated puffe cereal*
- *½ cup coarsely chopped hazelnuts*

Cream sugar and shortening. Add egg and vanilla an blend. Sift flour and measure. Sift again with baking powde and salt and add to creamed mixture. Add cereal and choppe hazelnuts. Drop from teaspoon onto greased cooky sheet Bake in a moderately hot oven (375°) 10 to 12 minutes.

Makes 40 cookies.

HAZELNUT YULE BARS

- *½ cup brown sugar, firmly packed*
- *½ cup butter*
- *1 cup sifted flour*
- *2 eggs, well beaten*
- *½ cup brown sugar, firmly packed*
- *½ cup corn syrup*
- *1 teaspoon vanilla*
- *2 tablespoons flour*
- *1 teaspoon baking powder*
- *½ teaspoon salt*
- *1 cup coarsely chopped hazelnuts*

Blend ½ cup of brown sugar and butter. Stir in flour. Pa out mixture in bottom of an ungreased pan (9×9×2 inches) Bake in a moderate oven (350°) for 20 minutes. Meanwhil blend eggs and remaining ½ cup of brown sugar. Stir in cor syrup and vanilla. Add flour, baking powder and salt, mixin well. Stir in hazelnuts and pour over bottom layer. Return to oven and bake 25–30 minutes longer or until top is golden brown. Cool in pan, cut into finger-length bars.

Makes 24 bars.

NOELS

1 *cup coarsely chopped hazelnuts, toasted*
1 *cup mixed candied fruits*
1 *cup grated coconut*
1 *cup butter or margarine*
1 *cup sugar*
1 *cup brown sugar, firmly packed*
½ *teaspoon salt*
1 *teaspoon vanilla*
2 *eggs*
2 *cups sifted flour*
1 *teaspoon baking powder*
1 *teaspoon soda*
2 *cups rolled oats*

Combine hazelnuts, candied fruits and coconut. Set aside. Cream butter or margarine with sugars until light and fluffy. Add salt, vanilla and eggs; beat well. Stir in the nuts, fruit and coconut. Sift the dry ingredients together and add to the rolled oats; add to the creamed mixture. Shape into 1-inch balls and drop onto cooky sheet; flatten with a fork and bake in a moderate oven (350°) 12 to 15 minutes.

Makes about 8½ dozen.

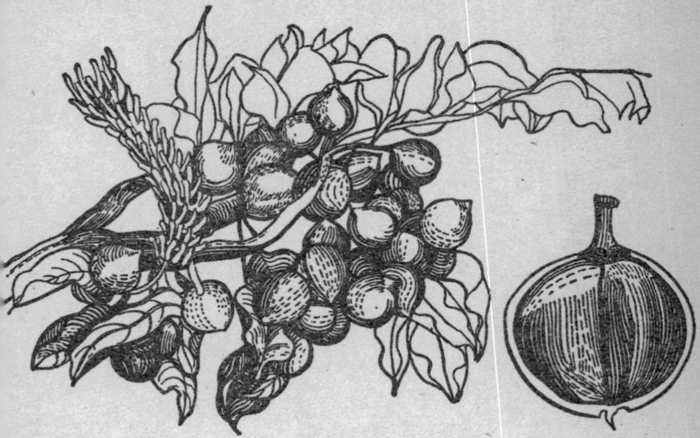

MACADAMIA NUTS

THE MACADAMIA NUT

Native to Australia, where it is known as the Australian bush, popple or bauple nut or by its aborigine name *kindal kindal*, the macadamia nut has taken on its true importance only since its introduction into Hawaii, where it has been seriously cultivated since 1892.

It is certain that this nut was much used by the aborigines before the date 1870, when it became generally known in Australia. The tree was planted by early settlers because of both its shade and its nuts. It is extraordinarily pretty, having a shiny foliage and bearing cream-colored or pink blossoms.

The wild tree generally reaches a height of 50 feet and branches fully from the base of the tree. The nuts ripen about 6 months after flowering, and during its bearing life each tree averages 50 to 100 pounds of nuts.

The macadamia has grown in popularity as its production in Hawaii has increased, and it is in great demand as a dessert nut. The kernels are hard to procure, growing in a tough brown shell up to ½ inch in thickness, which is in turn encased in a fibrous husk which must be removed by dehydration processes and submission to a cracking machine that grades, cracks and sorts these tasty morsels. Unlike most other nuts, the macadamia does not have a skin or thin outer covering (pellicle), but resembles a clean-shaven overgrown filbert. The macadamia is delicious combined with meats, fruits or fish. It is a favorite gourmet treat when served with beverages before or after dinner, and is a wholesome snack for any time of day when some quick energy is wanted.

RED SNAPPER QUEEN EMMA

4–5 pounds red snapper, whole
HAWAIIAN MACADAMIA NUT STUFFING
4 tomatoes, cut in halves
1 medium onion, sliced
¼ cup melted butter
1 cup dry white wine
2 bay leaves

Clean, split, and remove the bones from the red snapper. Season the fillets lightly with salt and pepper. Fill the inside cavity with Hawaiian Macadamia Nut Stuffing. Fasten the edges of the cavity with a trussing needle or toothpicks. Place in a lightly buttered baking pan. Place around the fish the halves of tomatoes, sprinkle with a little salt and pepper and place an onion slice on top of each one. Then brush the fish with melted butter. Add white wine and bay leaves and bake in a hot oven (400°) for 20 to 30 minutes or until fish is done. Garnish with lemon wedges, parsley, and stuffed eggs. Slice to serve.

Makes 8 to 10 servings.

HAWAIIAN MACADAMIA NUT STUFFING

3 cups day-old bread crumbs
1 cup coarsely chopped macadamia nuts
¼ cup melted butter
Juice of ½ lemon
Salt, pepper, pinch nutmeg

Combine bread crumbs, nuts, and melted butter. Season with salt, pepper, nutmeg, and lemon juice. Mix well.

BAKED CHICKEN IN MACADAMIA NUT CREAM

3 broiler-fryer chickens, halved
Salt and pepper
½ cup finely chopped macadamia nuts
½ cup flour
6 teaspoons butter
1 cup light cream (or half milk and cream)

Season chicken halves with salt and pepper. Place in a buttered baking pan. Combine the chopped nuts with flour and sprinkle over the chickens. Put a teaspoon of butter on each half and cover them with cream. Let stand in refrigerator several hours. Three quarters of an hour before serving, set the baking pan with the chicken in a hot oven (400°) about 15 minutes or until well browned. At the end of 15 minutes reduce the temperature to 350°. Cover the pan tightly and continue to cook for another half hour. The cream will be absorbed by the chicken while baking. If necessary, add additional cream during the baking period.

Makes 6 servings.

MACADAMIA NUT CREAMED CHICKEN

1 can (3 or 4 ounces) sliced mushrooms
1 cup chicken broth
⅓ cup butter
5 tablespoons flour
½ teaspoon salt
1 teaspoon paprika
1 cup milk
½ cup finely chopped macadamia nuts
2 cups diced cooked chicken

Drain liquid from mushrooms and add enough chicken broth to make 1 cup. Melt butter in saucepan. Blend in flour, salt, and paprika. Gradually add mushroom-chicken liquid and milk. Cook, stirring constantly, until mixture thickens and comes to a boil. Stir in macadamia nuts and chicken. Heat to serving temperature. Serve over toast points or hot cooked rice.

Makes 4 servings.

CHICKEN QUEEN KAPIOLANI

1 *broiler-fryer chicken, cut in serving pieces*
1 *teaspoon salt*
⅛ *teaspoon pepper*
6 *tablespoons butter*
1 *pound cooking apples, pared, cored, and thickly sliced*
1 *teaspoon sugar*
1 *cup coarsely chopped macadamia nuts*
½ *cup cider liqueur or apple cider*

Sprinkle chicken with salt and pepper. Brown in butter in skillet. Transfer to large casserole; top with apple slices. Sprinkle with the sugar and macadamia nuts. Add the cider liqueur. Cover the dish and bake in a moderately hot oven (375°). Cook until chicken is done (about 40 to 45 minutes).

Makes 6 servings.

FRIED SHRIMP MACADAMIA

1 *pound large fresh shrimp*
1 *large onion*
3 *whole cloves*
1 *whole lemon*
Sprigs of parsley
Salt and pepper
1½ *cups finely grated macadamia nuts*
2 *eggs, beaten*
Oil for frying

Place shrimp in boiling water to cover with the onion stuck with the cloves, lemon cut in half, several sprigs parsley and pinch of salt and pepper. When water returns to full boil, cook 5 minutes. Drain. When cooked, remove the shells from the shrimp and carefully remove black line from the backs. Dip each shrimp separately in finely grated macadamia nuts, then in the beaten egg and again in the macadamia nuts. Fry in deep fat (365°) until golden brown. Drain on absorbent paper. Serve with curry-flavored mayonnaise.

Makes 4 servings.

MACADAMIA NUT POTATO PUFFS

6 medium-size potatoes, cooked
½ cup milk
1 large egg
4 tablespoons butter
½ cup finely chopped macadamia nuts
2 teaspoons baking powder
2 teaspoons salt
¼ teaspoon white pepper

Press the cooked potatoes through a fine ricer, or mash them well. Add milk, egg, butter, macadamia nuts and baking powder. Stir well. Season with salt and pepper. Drop by large spoonfuls on a well-greased baking sheet and bake in a moderately hot oven (375°) 10 to 15 minutes.

Pressing the potato puffs mixture through a pastry bag will result in a very attractive arrangement.

Makes 8 servings.

MACADAMIA NUT WILD RICE STUFFING

1½ cups wild rice
¼ cup diced bacon, uncooked
2 tablespoons finely chopped onions
½ pound chopped mushrooms
⅓ cup melted butter
2 tablespoons minced parsley
½ teaspoon marjoram
½ teaspoon poultry seasoning
½ cup coarsely chopped macadamia nuts

Cook rice according to package directions. Drain and return to pot. Shake dry over low heat. Cook bacon in skillet until crisp. Add to wild rice. Add chopped onions to bacon drippings and fry until lightly browned. Add to rice. Sauté mushrooms in butter. Add to rice with minced parsley, marjoram, poultry seasoning, and the macadamia nuts.

The stuffing will be sufficient to stuff 6 squabs, 1 roasting chicken or capon, or 6 rock Cornish hens.

FROZEN PINEAPPLE AND MACADAMIA NUT SALAD

2 3-ounce packages cream cheese
1 cup mayonnaise
½ cup heavy cream, whipped
1 cup chopped macadamia nuts
¼ cup sugar
1 9-ounce can pineapple tidbits
½ cup chopped brandy-flavored maraschino cherries
Crisp lettuce leaves

Cream the cheese with 2 tablespoons of the mayonnaise until smooth. Add remaining mayonnaise, whipped cream, and blend well. Mix in the chopped macadamia nuts, sugar and fruits. Pack in a mold and freeze, or put in refrigerator tray and freeze. Serve on crisp lettuce leaves.

Makes 8 to 10 servings.

MACADAMIA NUT PUMPKIN PIE

½ cup sugar
1 cup brown sugar, firmly packed
½ teaspoon ginger
¼ teaspoon cloves
1 teaspoon cinnamon
Pinch of salt
1 cup cooked pumpkin
1 cup milk, scalded
2 eggs, slightly beaten
1 cup very finely chopped macadamia nuts
1 unbaked 9-inch pie shell

Mix ingredients in order given. Turn into unbaked pie shell. Bake in a hot oven (425°) for 15 minutes, then lower the heat to 350° and bake 35 minutes or until custard is set.

Makes 1 9-inch pie.

MACADAMIA NUT BOURBON MARVELS

1 *cup vanilla wafer crumbs*
1 *cup finely chopped macadamia nuts*
2 *tablespoons cocoa*
¼ *cup bourbon*
1¼ *tablespoons white corn syrup*
1 *cup sifted confectioners' sugar*

Combine crumbs, nuts and cocoa. Blend bourbon and corn syrup together and add to dry ingredients. Blend thoroughly and form into 1-inch balls. Roll in powdered sugar and chill in refrigerator.

Makes about 18 balls.

BUTTERSCOTCH MACADAMIA NUT PIE

1 *cup brown sugar, firmly packed*
¼ *cup water*
¼ *cup butter*
1 *tablespoon light corn syrup*
½ *cup sugar*
3 *tablespoons cornstarch*
3 *tablespoons flour*
¼ *tablespoon salt*
1½ *cups scalded milk*
2 *egg yolks, beaten*
1 *baked 9-inch pie shell*
1½ *cups chopped macadamia nuts*
Whipped cream

Cook the brown sugar, water, butter and syrup together to a soft-ball stage (238°). Mix the sugar, cornstarch, flour, salt and milk in the top of a double boiler and cook 15 minutes, stirring constantly until thick and smooth. Add small amount of mixture to beaten egg yolks, mixing well. Return to double boiler and cook for 2 minutes. Remove from heat and beat in the brown-sugar syrup. Pour into baked pie shell. Sprinkle top with chopped macadamia nuts and cool. Cover with whipped cream, then again sprinkle the top with a layer of chopped macadamia nuts.

Makes 1 9-inch pie.

PEANUTS

THE PEANUT

Native to Peru and Brazil and cultivated there by the pre-Columbian Indians, the peanut reached the United States by long, circuitous route, returning to the shores of this hemisphere via Africa, where it was introduced by early explorers nd Portuguese slave traders who used the peanut as rations n their ships. First planted around the doorways of slave abins, the peanut, being immune to most agricultural disases, developed into a cash crop when "King Cotton" was truck down by the boll weevil. Its use was noted by Union oldiers of the Civil War, who carried some of these delicious ground peas" (for that is what peanuts really are) home vith them and thus started the Northern hunger for this asty and nutritious food, noted in later days for the quick nergy it supplies at circuses and baseball games.

Humans, animals and birds all adore this product of the arth, which is so important to the agriculture and economy f the South that Congress has declared it to be one of our ation's six basic crops.

Americans consume about 500 tons annually, and that is nly 10 per cent of the crop of the world. However, peanuts re used in more ways in the United States than in the rest of the world, where they are grown mainly for their oil. In countries other than ours millions of lives might be saved if only the problem of converting and distributing huge peanut crops into foodstuffs could be solved as it has been in our land.

The peanut is an easy crop to grow. It thrives well in hot climates with well-defined wet and dry seasons. It is an annual. As its flowers develop, the male buds drop off while the female flowers elongate, bend to touch the ground, and eventually penetrate the soil where the nuts as we know them begin to shape and grow.

Harvesting is done by loosening the plants in the soil and pulling them up, with the nuts still holding tight to the stalks of the plant. Machines are used in every part of the process necessary to dig, pick, clean, separate, grade, inspect, shell and package peanuts, although the nuts used for confectionery purposes are distinctly referred to as "H.P.S."—Hand Picked Selected—for such they are.

The percentage of oil and protein peanuts contain makes them very important as a food to be used for flesh and muscle formation. In Africa and India peanuts are frequently used as a substitute for meats and in curries, and in India many sweetmeats are made in which peanuts are used.

Many by-products of the peanut have been developed (notably by the late George Washington Carver of Tuskegee Institute), but actually half of our edible domestic crop is diverted to the manufacture of our famous peanut butter (which can rival the steak in food value) while the other parts of the crop go into confections, candy production and dozens of quick-energy snacks, as well as into those bags of tasty roasted nuts which are an American legend.

Today the nutrition of the peanut is readily available to all. How wise the homemaker who adds muscle-building protein to her family meals by combining the foods she serves with some form of this health-giving nut of the earth—the peanut!

SPICED PEANUTS

1½ cups blanched peanuts
2 cups sifted confectioners' sugar
½ cup cornstarch
2 teaspoons salt
1 teaspoon nutmeg
¼ cup cinnamon
2 teaspoons ginger
1 tablespoon ground cloves
1 egg white
2 tablespoons cold water

Sift together three times the sugar, cornstarch, salt and spices. Beat egg white slightly and add the cold water. Put the peanuts in a wire strainer and dip into the egg mixture until each nut is well coated. Drain. Roll the peanuts in a part of the spice mixture. Spread the spice mixture one fourth inch thick in a shallow pan and place the peanuts on this, separating each one. Cover with the rest of the spice mixture and bake in a very slow oven (250°) 2 hours. Remove from the oven and sift. Save the spice mixture to use again.

NUT BUTTER

2 cups blanched roasted peanuts
1 tablespoon peanut oil
½ teaspoon salt (optional)

Put peanuts through food chopper twice, using finest blade. If too coarse, put paste through again. Add oil and salt and mix well. Keep in tightly covered glass jar.

Makes about ½ pound.

Variations: Almonds, cashews, pecans or other nuts may be substituted. Use cottonseed or other tasteless oil in place of peanut oil.

PEANUT CHEESE BALL

½ pound roquefort cheese
2 ounces blue cheese
2 3-ounce packages cream cheese
¼ cup finely minced onions
½ cup chopped parsley
1½ teaspoons Worcestershire sauce
1 cup chopped roasted peanuts

Blend all ingredients except ½ cup of the peanuts. Chill. When slightly hardened, shape into a ball. Roll in remaining nuts. Serve with crackers or bite-size whole-wheat biscuits.

Makes about 3 cups.

CREAM OF PEANUT BUTTER SOUP

2 celery tops
1¼ cups water
1 teaspoon salt
2 tablespoons butter
1 tablespoon minced onions
½ cup minced celery
2 tablespoons flour
3 tablespoons peanut butter
2 cups milk
Pepper
Paprika

Cook celery tops in the water and salt about 10 minutes. Strain and reserve water. Melt butter, add onions and celery. Cook for two minutes. Stir in flour. Add peanut butter after flour has been well blended. Stir in milk and celery water. Stir over low heat until mixture boils. Season to taste with pepper. Sprinkle with paprika when ready to serve.

Makes 4 to 6 servings.

PEANUT PATCH CORN CHOWDER

1½ cups finely sliced onions
3 tablespoons peanut oil
1 tablespoon salt
2 cups boiling water
1 quart diced raw potatoes
¼ teaspoon hot pepper sauce
1 cup crunchy peanut butter
1 16-ounce can whole kernel corn
5 cups milk
3 tablespoons diced pimiento
2 tablespoons frozen chopped chives

In large saucepan or deep skillet simmer onions in peanut oil, stirring frequently, until just tender. Do not brown. Add salt, water, diced potatoes and hot pepper sauce. Boil 15 minutes until potatoes are just tender. Blend a little of the hot soup with the peanut butter; stir mixture into soup. Add corn and milk. Heat just to simmering. Serve in tureen or bowls. Sprinkle with pimiento and chives.

Makes 8–10 servings.

GOLDEN PEANUT CHEDDA BISQUE

½ cup finely chopped celery
½ cup grated raw carrot
1 cup boiling water
2 tablespoons peanut oil
⅓ cup flour
1 teaspoon salt
2 cups milk
1 10½-ounce can beef broth
½ pound sharp Cheddar cheese, grated
¾ cup crunchy peanut butter
Toasted sesame seeds

In small saucepan, simmer celery and carrots in boiling water until tender. Combine peanut oil, flour, and salt in large saucepan over low heat; gradually stir in milk. Stir until thickened. Add cooked vegetables and their liquid, beef broth and grated cheese. Heat to boiling, stirring occasionally. Mix a little of hot liquid with peanut butter; stir mixture into soup. Simmer 5 minutes. Serve in tureen or bowls, sprinkled with toasted sesame seeds.

Makes 4 to 6 servings.

PEANUT-CRESS SOUP POT WITH SAVORY TOASTED PEANUTS

- 1 *bunch watercress*
- 4 *chicken bouillon cubes*
- 4 *cups water*
- 2 *tablespoons peanut oil*
- ⅓ *cup flour*
- 1½ *teaspoons salt*
- ⅛ *teaspoon pepper*
- 1 *tall can* (1⅔ *cups*) *evaporated milk*
- 1 *cup creamy peanut butter*
- *Few sprigs watercress*
- ¾ *cup salted peanut halves*
- 1 *tablespoon peanut oil*
- *Seasoning salt*

Put cleaned watercress, including stems, through finest blade of food chopper. Combine with bouillon cubes and water in large saucepan. Bring to a boil, stirring until bouillon cubes are dissolved. Simmer 10 minutes. Combine 2 tablespoons peanut oil with flour, salt and pepper. Gradually blend in part of evaporated milk to make thin, creamy mixture. Slowly add to hot soup, stirring until soup comes to a boil. Add remaining evaporated milk. Blend a little of hot mixture with peanut butter; add to hot soup, stirring until well blended. Bring just to a boil. Serve in tureen or bowls, spangled with minced watercress sprigs. Pass hot Savory Toasted Peanuts for a crunchy topping, with crisp melba toast rounds as accompaniment.

Makes 6–8 servings.

SAVORY TOASTED PEANUTS: In small skillet, stir salted peanut halves with 1 tablespoon peanut oil over low heat for two minutes. Drain on paper towel and dust with seasoning salt. Keep hot.

PEANUT LAND'S SHANGHAI SPECIAL

½ pound veal or pork, diced
2 teaspoons shortening
3 cups chopped celery
1 cup minced onions
2 cups chopped salted peanuts
1 cup water
⅛ teaspoon pepper
2 tablespoons soy or meat sauce
Salt
3 cups hot cooked rice

Brown meat in shortening in skillet. Add celery, onions, peanuts, water, pepper and sauce. Cover tightly and simmer 30 to 45 minutes. Salt to taste. Serve over hot rice.

Makes 6 servings.

NUTBURGERS

6 slices bacon
1½ pounds ground beef
1 teaspoon salt
6 tablespoons chopped peanuts
3 tablespoons chopped parsley
2 tablespoons grated onion

Sauté bacon until lightly browned. Season beef with salt and divide into 12 *portions*. Shape into thin cakes. Make a filling, using the chopped peanuts, parsley and onion. Spread on 6 of the cakes. Cover each with slice of bacon, cut in half. Top with the 6 remaining cakes. Pinch edges together. Broil the nutburgers about 5 minutes on first side, turn and broil 4 minutes on second side. May also be pan-broiled.

Makes 6 Nutburgers.

STUFFED HAM SLICES

2 cups fine soft bread crumbs
½ cup seedless raisins
⅓ cup unsalted roasted peanuts, chopped
2 tablespoons dark corn syrup
½ teaspoon dry mustard
1 tablespoon butter, melted
2 slices ready-to-eat smoked ham, ½ inch thick (about 1½ pounds)
PEANUT BUTTER-RAISIN SAUCE

Combine all ingredients except ham. Place one slice of ham in shallow pan with tight-fitting lid; spread stuffing over first slice and top with the other. Stick whole cloves in ham. Bake covered in a moderate oven (350°) for 30 minutes; remove cover and bake 15 minutes longer. Serve with Peanut Butter-Raisin Sauce.

Makes 6 servings.

PEANUT BUTTER-RAISIN SAUCE

¼ cup honey
½ cup water
⅓ cup raisins
¼ teaspoon salt
⅓ cup peanut butter

Combine honey, water, raisins and salt. Bring quickly to a boil and boil 2 minutes. Cool. Place peanut butter in small bowl of mixer, add syrup gradually, beating with electric mixer until smooth. Store in covered jar in refrigerator until ready to use. Delicious over ice cream, puddings, cake, and meats.

SAUCY STUFFED HAM WITH PEANUT-APPLE BUTTER GLAZE

5- to 6-pound canned ham, or 3 center-cut ham slices ½ inch thick

FRUITY NUT DRESSING

4 cups ½-inch bread cubes
½ cup corn meal
1 cup finely diced celery
1 cup finely diced raw apple
½ cup raisins
1½ teaspoons salt
¼ teaspoon pepper
¼ cup melted butter or margarine
½ cup crunchy peanut butter
Hot water to moisten

PEANUT-APPLE BUTTER GLAZE

½ cup creamy peanut butter
1 cup maple syrup
¾ cup apple butter
½ teaspoon cream of tartar
1 cup salted peanuts, coarsely chopped

If canned ham is used, have butcher cut it horizontally into three equal slices. If ham slices are used, slash fat around edges to prevent curling. Place first ham slice on large piece of heavy-duty foil. Combine nut dressing ingredients, tossing lightly with enough hot water to moisten. Pile half of dressing in even layer to cover ham slice. Put second ham slice in place, then remaining dressing topped with third ham slice. Press together firmly. Bring foil up snugly around ham, sealing it across top. Bake in a slow oven (325°) 2 hours.

In saucepan combine all glaze ingredients except peanuts. Simmer, stirring constantly, until well blended and hot. Add peanuts. During the last 30 minutes of baking time, open foil around top of ham and baste with the glaze several times, reserving approximately 1 cup.

To serve, remove ham to hot platter. For sauce, combine drippings with remaining glaze, thinning with maple syrup if desired. To carve, slice down through ham and dressing. Reheat sauce and pass.

Makes 16 to 20 servings.

PEANUT BUTTER PORKIES

6 double pork chops
1 8-ounce package seasoned stuffing
½ cup crunchy peanut butter
1 cup dried apricots, chopped
½ teaspoon salt
Hot water or broth to moisten

Have pocket cut in each double pork chop. Combine remaining ingredients, tossing until well blended, then fill pockets in pork chops. Heat peanut oil or drippings in large deep skillet and brown chops on both sides. Cover and continue simmering over low heat 1 hour, adding a little water if needed and turning once during cooking time. Remove chops and make cream gravy from drippings.

Makes 6 servings.

LOUISIANA ROAST DUCK

6-pound duck
Salt, pepper, garlic clove
4 cups stale or toasted bread, small pieces or cubed
1 cup chopped celery
1 cup chopped onions
½ teaspoon salt
¼ teaspoon pepper
½ cup milk, scalded
1 cup peanut butter

Wash and clean duck; rub with salt, pepper and garlic clove. Mix bread, celery, onions, salt and pepper. Add scalded milk to peanut butter in separate bowl, mix until blended. Add dry bread mixture and mix thoroughly. Fill neck and body cavities with stuffing and close openings with poultry pins or by sewing.

Place duck on rack in open pan and roast 20 to 30 minutes per pound at an oven temperature of 325°. Place foil over top for self-basting. Remove foil 30 minutes before duck is finished.

A quicker way to make the stuffing is to use prepared dry stuffing and simply add the scalded milk and peanut butter. This, however, retains the herb flavors of the prepared stuffing, which somewhat neutralize the subtle peanut flavor.

Makes 4 servings.

BAKED CHICKEN SALAD WITH PEANUTS

2 *cups diced cooked chicken*
2 *cups thinly sliced celery*
½ *cup chopped peanuts*
2 *teaspoons minced onion*
1 *teaspoon salt*
1 *cup mayonnaise*
2 *tablespoons lemon juice*
½ *cup grated cheese*
1 *cup finely crushed potato chips*

Combine ingredients except cheese and potato chips. Pile lightly in casserole or individual baking dishes, sprinkle with cheese and potato chips. Bake in a hot oven (400°) 25 minutes.

Makes 4 servings.

NUT ROAST

3 tablespoons butter
1 onion, minced
1 green pepper, chopped
1 cup cooked rice
⅓ cup bread crumbs
1 cup tomatoes
1 tablespoon Worcestershire sauce
1 cup peanuts, chopped
1 egg, beaten
2 tablespoons chopped parsley
¾ teaspoon salt
1 teaspoon onion salt
1 teaspoon celery salt

Melt butter in skillet. Sauté onion and green pepper until soft. Combine all ingredients and place in a greased casserole. Bake in a moderately hot oven (375°) 30 minutes. Serve at once.

Makes 4 servings.

FRUIT-NUT COLE SLAW

1 medium cabbage
2 diced, unpeeled red apples
1 cup drained pineapple chunks
½ cup salted peanuts
Salt to taste
½ cup mayonnaise

Shred cabbage; toss with diced apple, pineapple chunks, peanuts, salt and mayonnaise. Serve in salad bowl.

Makes 6 servings.

FROZEN PEANUT SALAD

2 3-ounce packages cream cheese
½ teaspoon salt
½ cup mayonnaise
Juice of 1 lemon
½ cup crushed pineapple, drained
2 bananas, sliced
½ cup maraschino cherries
½ cup salted peanuts, chopped
1 cup cream, lightly whipped
Crisp salad greens
Peanuts

Mix cream cheese, salt, mayonnaise and lemon juice; add fruit, peanuts, and fold in cream. Pour in cold freezing tray and freeze until firm with control set at coldest position. Slice, serve with favorite salad greens and dressing. Garnish with whole peanuts.

Makes 6 servings.

PEANUT BUTTER YEAST LOAF

¾ cup milk, scalded
¼ cup sugar
⅓ cup creamy peanut butter
1½ teaspoons salt
1 package active dry yeast
¼ cup lukewarm water
1 egg, slightly beaten
3½ cups sifted flour
½ cup finely chopped peanuts
1 egg white, slightly beaten
2 tablespoons peanut halves

Thoroughly blend hot milk with sugar, peanut butter and salt; cool to lukewarm. Stir yeast into lukewarm water until dissolved; add egg, mix well. Stir into lukewarm peanut-butter mixture. Add half the flour; beat well. Beat in remaining flour. Knead on lightly floured board until smooth and elastic, from 7 to 10 minutes. Place in greased bowl, turning over once to grease dough lightly. Cover and let rise in warm place (80° to 85°) 2 hours. Punch down, cover and let rise until half again its original size (about ½ hour). Punch down and knead in ½ cup finely chopped peanuts. Mold into loaf and place in greased 8½×4½×2½-inch loaf pan. Cover with towel and let rise until double in size (about 2 hours). Bake in a moderately hot oven (375°) 25 to 30 minutes or until well browned. Remove from oven, brush with egg white and scatter with peanut halves, pressing them lightly against glaze. Return to oven for 3 minutes. Cool before slicing.

Makes 1 loaf.

SPICED APPLE PEANUT MUFFINS

2 cups flour
3 teaspoons baking powder
⅓ cup sugar
½ teaspoon salt
½ teaspoon nutmeg
½ teaspoon cinnamon
1 egg
¾ cup milk
4 tablespoons peanut oil
1 cup diced raw apples
½ cup salted peanuts, coarsely ground

Sift dry ingredients. Beat egg, add milk and add to dry mixture. Add peanut oil and fold in diced apples and peanuts. Fill greased muffin tins two thirds full. Bake in a hot oven (400°) 20 to 30 minutes.

Makes 1 dozen muffins.

PEANUT WAFFLES

4 cups sifted flour
5 teaspoons baking powder
1 tablespoon sugar
1½ teaspoons salt
¾ cup peanuts, chopped
4 eggs
2 cups milk
⅓ cup peanut oil

Sift flour with baking powder, sugar and salt. Stir chopped peanuts into flour mixture. Beat eggs. Add milk and peanut oil. Add to dry ingredients all at one time and stir until just mixed. Bake on hot waffle iron according to manufacturer's instructions. Serve with butter and syrup, topped with fruit or ice cream, or used as a base for creamed chicken or fish.

Makes 12 to 15 waffles.

APPLE DATE BREAD

1 egg
1 cup applesauce
2 tablespoons peanut oil
2 cups sifted flour
¾ cup sugar
3 teaspoons baking powder
½ teaspoon cinnamon
¼ teaspoon allspice
½ teaspoon soda
¾ cup chopped peanuts
½ cup chopped dates

Beat egg lightly in mixing bowl and stir in applesauce and peanut oil. Sift dry ingredients together; mix in chopped peanuts and dates. Add to egg mixture, stirring just enough to blend. Turn into well-greased 9×5×3-inch loaf pan (or use a narrow pan). Bake in a moderate oven (350°) 60 to 70 minutes until done. For a pretty topping, brush hot top crust with egg white and decorate with salted peanut halves. Return to oven for three minutes. Cool in pans 10 minutes; turn out on rack and cool completely. Wrap in foil or wax paper and store overnight before slicing. Slice thin.
Makes 1 loaf.

BANANA NUT BREAD

½ cup shortening
1 cup sugar
2 eggs
1 cup mashed bananas (3 to 4 fully ripe)
1 teaspoon lemon juice
2 cups sifted flour
3 teaspoons baking powder
½ teaspoon salt
1 cup chopped roasted peanuts

Cream shortening and sugar. Beat eggs well and add. Add lemon juice to mashed bananas and mix into the creamed mixture. Sift flour, baking powder, and salt together and add; add peanuts. Turn into greased loaf pan. Bake in a moderately hot oven (375°) 50 minutes.
Makes 1 loaf.

PEANUT BRITTLE CRISPS

½ cup shortening
⅔ cup sugar
2 eggs, well beaten
1¾ cups sifted flour
1 teaspoon baking powder
½ teaspoon salt
¼ teaspoon allspice
½ teaspoon cinnamon
¼ cup milk
1 cup finely chopped peanut brittle

Cream shortening, add sugar gradually. Beat in eggs. Sift together flour, baking powder, salt, allspice and cinnamon.

Add alternately with milk to first mixture. Stir in peanu brittle. Drop by heaping teaspoonfuls on greased cooky shee Flatten slightly with spatula. Bake in a moderately hot ove (375°) 10 minutes or until cookies are golden brown.

Makes 3 dozen cookies.

PEANUT BROWNIES

1 cup sugar
¼ teaspoon salt
2 eggs
2 squares baking chocolate, melted
½ teaspoon vanilla
¼ cup peanut oil
¾ cup sifted flour
½ cup chopped peanuts

Blend sugar, salt, eggs, chocolate and vanilla. Add peanu oil alternately with flour to sugar mixture. Stir in choppe peanuts. Spread batter into well-oiled 8-inch square pan. Bak in a moderate oven (350°) 30 minutes. Cut in squares whe partially cool.

Makes 16 brownies.

PEANUT CRUNCH COOKIES

1 cup sifted flour
1 teaspoon baking powder
½ teaspoon salt
⅓ cup soft shortening
⅓ cup sugar
⅓ cup brown sugar, firmly packed
¼ cup peanut butter
1 egg
½ teaspoon vanilla
½ cup chopped peanuts

Sift flour, add baking powder and salt and sift togethe Mix shortening with sugars, add peanut butter, egg and va nilla and cream until light. Mix in flour mixture, then pe nuts. Chill till easy to handle. Shape dough into small ball place on greased cooky sheet, flatten with fork. Bake in a moderate oven (350°) 12 to 15 minutes.

Makes approximately 4 dozen cookies.

PEANUT CRUNCH PIE

1 unbaked 9-inch pastry shell
¼ cup sugar
1 tablespoon quick-cooking tapioca
¼ teaspoon salt
1 cup dark corn syrup
¼ cup water
3 eggs
½ teaspoon vanilla
2 tablespoons butter or margarine
1 cup peanuts, coarsely chopped

Prepare pastry shell but do not bake. Blend sugar, tapioca and salt in a medium-size saucepan. Stir in corn syrup and water. Bring to a boil, stirring constantly. Boil 4 minutes. Beat eggs slightly. Pour hot syrup slowly into eggs, stirring vigorously. Stir in vanilla and butter. Cool. Scatter chopped peanuts over bottom of pastry shell. Add cooled pie filling. Bake in a hot oven (450°) 8 minutes. Reduce heat to 325° and bake 25 to 35 minutes, or until a silver knife inserted in the center comes out clean. Serve warm, or cool and top with sweetened whipped cream.

Makes 1 9-inch pie.

PEANUT BRITTLE ICE CREAM

1 cup finely crushed peanut brittle
Pinch of salt
1⅓ cups light cream
2 eggs, separated
1 cup heavy cream
1 teaspoon vanilla

Add the peanut brittle and salt to the light cream and stir until blended. Beat the egg whites until stiff. Beat egg yolks until thick and lemon-colored. Beat heavy cream until thick but not stiff; add the vanilla. Combine all ingredients and mix well. Pour into freezing tray of automatic refrigerator and freeze, with temperature at coldest setting. Stir once during freezing.

Makes 6 servings.

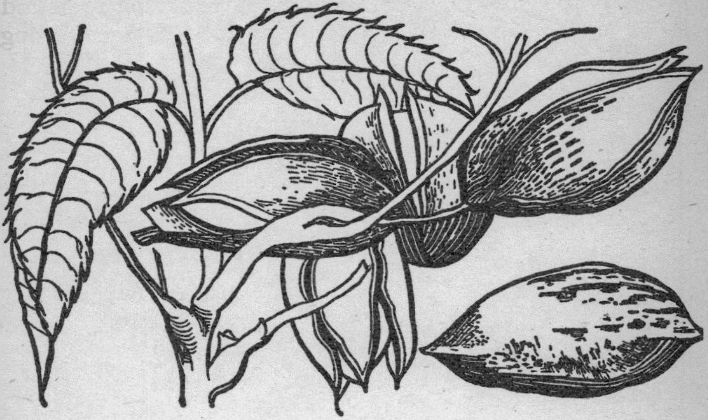

PECANS

THE PECAN

Did you know that man could subsist for a long period of time on pecans alone? Well, it's true. The Spanish explorer de Vaca tells us, in the log of his adventures, of Indians who survived two months of the year by eating "walnuts" alone. So rich in nutritional benefits are these nuts from the hickory tree that the Indians stored them up against the food scarcities of winter. The Creeks in particular were accustomed to pounding the kernels to pieces, after which they would throw them in boiling water, pass them through fine strainers, and finally extract a rich, creamy liquid which they called "hickory milk" and which they used in the making of their hominy and corncakes.

The name pecan comes from the Indian word for the nut which was very similar in all the Indian dialects, being known in the Cree and Algonquian as *paccan*; in the Ojibway as *pagan*; in the Abnaki as *pagann*. The meaning of the word is "nut having hard shell to crack."

The pecan is completely American. Its usefulness was quickly discovered by our early settlers, and in its native range (from Illinois and Ohio down the Mississippi and extending through New Mexico and Texas) its bounty was so great that it precluded the necessity of planting, although both George Washington and Thomas Jefferson, who loved these nuts, made purposeful plantings of the pecan on their estates which still exist.

The wild forest tree is known as the Seedling Pecan. It has become a commercial crop, still growing wild along the river bottoms as in Indian days. The trees grow unattended and uncultivated for the most part, though some have been marked out in well-managed, productive groves from which come small pecans, delicious in flavor with a firm full kernel especially adaptable for commercial uses. A major crop of these nuts is produced in alternate years, a characteristic which persists even in the cultivated varieties despite years of research and study. This is due to faulty pollination every other year.

There is no definite record of the first planting of cultivated pecans for commercial purposes, but our large superb orchards of today got their start in 1846–47 when Antoine, a slave gardener on Oak Alley Plantation in Louisiana, became the first to graft pecan trees successfully. He worked on his project until, at the end of the Civil War, he was known to have created 126 trees of the variety from which the famous "centennial" pecans have been the result. Careful grafting or budding of the trees and dedicated research in the techniques of growing and cultivation have been carried on to produce the "paper-shell" pecans of today, which have a much meatier kernel inside a shell which is easier to crack than that of the Seedling Pecan. Cultivated and Seedling pecans are both harvested from late October into the early winter months by three different methods: *natural,* letting the mature nuts fall to the ground from the force of wind or rain; *knocking* by hand to loosen the nuts from the tree; *mechanical shaking* by use of a machine which brings the nuts down.

From grove to consumer the quality of the pecans is carefully guarded. They are put through a series of highly mechanized operations which include cracking, shelling, picking, grading, drying, polishing, and packaging, all of which takes several days. In shell, pecans may be stored at room temperature for prolonged periods of time, or they may be placed in the main section of the refrigerator the same as pecan kernels, which keep best in a covered glass jar.

Pecans are illustrious for the variety of ways in which they may be used in our favorite dishes. They may be added to drinks and dips, toasted to garnish soups, added to stuffings and sauces, used as toppings for casseroles, desserts, ice creams, custards, combined with packaged puddings and cakes, added to sandwich fillings or sprinkled on top of salads.

As early as 1721 Le Page du Pratz described pecans in these terms: "They are more delicate in flavor than our own [walnuts], less oily and so fine that the French make pralines of them as good as those made of almonds." Today the New Orleans praline is world-famous, a fitting monument to the one nut which grows *only* in the United States and represents to the world the practical bounty of the glorious wild larder which still exists in our land even in these days of development and mechanization.

PECAN SANDWICH SPREAD

½ cup finely chopped pecans
¼ cup finely chopped celery
¼ cup coarsely chopped stuffed olives
1½ tablespoons mayonnaise

Combine ingredients. Spread on lightly buttered thin slices of white or whole-wheat bread.

Makes about ¾ cup.

PECAN CHEESE MOLD

1 *large glass of Cheddar cheese spread*
1 *3-ounce package cream cheese*
½ teaspoon Worcestershire sauce
6 *or* 8 *stuffed olives, chopped*
1 *cup chopped pecans*

Have all ingredients at room temperature. Thoroughly blend the cheeses. Add sauce and olives. Make into a ball and roll in pecans. Chill and serve with crackers. (Best to make mold several days before serving to allow pecans to permeate cheese.)

Makes 1 small ball.

CURRIED PECANS

2 *tablespoons olive oil* (or *salad oil*)
¼ *teaspoon garlic powder*
½ *teaspoon salt*
2 *cups pecan halves*
¼ *teaspoon curry powder*

Combine olive oil, garlic powder and salt in a heavy skillet. Add nuts and toast over medium heat for 7 to 8 minutes, stirring constantly. When thoroughly heated, sprinkle with curry powder. Mix well. Serve hot.

Makes 2 cups.

PECAN HAM ROLL-UPS

2 *cups mashed sweet potatoes*
3 *tablespoons melted butter*
½ *cup crushed pineapple*
½ *cup fine dry bread crumbs*
3 *tablespoons sugar*
¼ *cup chopped pecans*
6 *slices boiled ham,* ⅛ *inch thick*
¾ *cup pineapple juice*

Combine sweet potatoes, butter, pineapple, crumbs, and sugar. Add pecans, and mix well. Spread this filling on the ham. Roll as for jelly roll, fasten with toothpicks, or tie. Place in baking dish and cover with pineapple juice. Bake in a moderate oven (350°) 20 minutes, basting frequently.

Makes 3 servings.

MEAT LOAF WITH PECAN STUFFING

1½ pounds ground beef
½ cup chopped green pepper
½ cup chopped onions
1 teaspoon salt
1 tablespoon Worcestershire sauce
1 cup white bread crumbs
½ cup milk
2 eggs
¼ cup butter
2 cups whole-wheat bread crumbs
½ cup chopped celery
¼ teaspoon black pepper
¾ cup meat stock or water
½ cup chopped pecans

Combine beef with green pepper, onions, salt, sauce, white bread crumbs, milk and 1 of the eggs. Mix thoroughly. Place half of this mixture in bottom of greased loaf pan. Combine remaining egg, butter, whole-wheat bread crumbs, celery, black pepper, meat stock or water, and chopped pecans. Spread on top of meat mixture. Arrange remaining meat mixture on top of pecan stuffing. Bake in a moderate oven (350°) 1½ hours and cool slightly before removing from pan.

Makes 10 servings.

PECAN-STUFFED PEPPERS

6 green peppers
1½ cups cooked rice
1½ cups chopped pecans
1½ teaspoons salt
¾ cup tomato juice
3 tablespoons shortening
2 pounds ground beef
1½ tablespoons minced onions
3 tablespoons finely chopped celery
¾ cup water or tomato juice

Parboil green peppers, which have been seeded and cored, until just tender enough to prick with a fork. Drain and keep warm. Make stuffing by combining rice, pecans, salt, and tomato juice. Sauté in shortening, beef, onions and celery. Mix meat mixture with rice mixture, stirring thoroughly but handling as little as possible. Stuff peppers and place in greased baking pan. Pour ¾ cup either water or tomato juice into pan around peppers. Bake in a moderate oven (350°) 30 minutes.

Makes 6 peppers.

PECAN WALDORF SALAD

- 1 *cup chopped apples, unpeeled*
- 2 *tablespoons chopped maraschino cherries*
- ½ *cup chopped pecans*
- ½ *cup diced celery*
- ½ *cup mayonnaise or salad dressing*

Mix fruit, pecans, celery and mayonnaise. Chill and serve on crisp lettuce leaves.

Makes 4 servings.

ROANOKE PECAN STUFFING FOR TURKEY, CAPON OR CHICKEN

- *Turkey, capon or roasting chicken*
- 2 *cups water*
- 2 *celery stalks, quartered*
- 1 *peeled carrot, cut into ½-inch slices*
- 1 *small onion, cut into quarters*
- ½ *teaspoon salt*
- 1 *cup butter or margarine*
- 2 *cups thinly sliced celery*
- 1 *cup chopped onions*
- ½ *cup finely chopped parsley*
- 1 *cup uncooked rice*
- 4 *cups small cornbread pieces*
- 2 *cups small torn whole-wheat bread pieces*
- 2 *cups chopped pecans*
- 2 *4-ounce cans mushroom stems and pieces, undrained*
- 3 *teaspoons poultry seasoning*
- 1½ *teaspoons salt*
- ½ *teaspoon pepper*

Combine neck and gizzard of turkey, capon or roasting chicken, water, stalks of celery, carrot slices, onion quarters and ½ teaspoon salt in saucepan; cover and simmer gently until gizzard is tender. Discard vegetables and neck and set stock aside to cool. Cut gizzard into small pieces.

Melt ½ cup of the butter or margarine in fry pan. Add sliced celery, chopped onions and parsley; cook over low heat until tender but not brown. Set aside. Brown rice in remaining ½ cup butter in fry pan or Dutch oven. Add enough water to poultry stock to make 3 cups liquid, and add to rice.

Simmer 20 minutes, stirring occasionally. In a large mixing bowl combine the breads, celery-onion mixture, rice and stock, pecans, mushrooms, seasonings; mix well. Season cavities of bird with salt; stuff loosely with dressing; skewer and roast as desired.

Makes 12 cups stuffing.

ORANGE PECAN SHORTBREAD

½ cup butter
⅓ cup sugar
2 egg yolks
1 teaspoon vanilla
1¼ cups sifted flour
¼ teaspoon soda
¼ teaspoon salt
1 cup orange marmalade
½ cup chopped pecans
2 egg whites, beaten stiff but not dry
1 tablespoon sugar
Pecan halves

Cream butter and sugar until fluffy. Add egg yolks and vanilla and beat well. Sift dry ingredients together and mix thoroughly, then add to butter mixture. Press into bottom and sides of 9-inch pie pan. Spread marmalade on shortbread to form a layer of filling. Sprinkle chopped pecans over marmalade. Spread beaten egg whites over nuts and marmalade. Arrange pecan halves on topping, then sprinkle with sugar. Bake in a moderate oven (350°) 30 minutes.

Makes 8 servings.

PECAN YEAST ROLLS

2 packages dry yeast
¼ cup lukewarm water
1 cup milk
¼ cup shortening
⅓ cup sugar
1 teaspoon salt
½ teaspoon grated lemon rind
2 eggs, beaten
5 cups sifted flour
⅓ cup melted butter or margarine
1 cup light brown sugar
1 cup chopped pecans
108 pecan halves

Soften yeast in lukewarm water. Scald milk and to it add the shortening, sugar, salt, and lemon rind. Cool to lukewarm. Stir in beaten eggs and softened yeast. Add half the flour and beat thoroughly. Add remaining flour and mix well. Turn out onto lightly floured board and knead lightly. Place in greased bowl; cover and set in warm place (80°–85°). Allow dough to rise until double in bulk. When light, punch down and turn out onto floured board. Roll dough in large rectangle about ½ inch thick. Spread with melted butter or margarine, brown sugar and chopped pecans. Roll jelly-roll fashion and cut in ¾-inch slices. Grease tins for 36 muffins, place 3 pecan halves in bottom of each and put a slice of the roll on top, cut side down. Allow to rise again until double in bulk. Then bake in a hot oven (400°) 15 to 18 minutes. *Makes 3 dozen.*

PECAN WHEAT BREAD

2 cups whole-wheat flour
2½ cups sifted flour
5 teaspoons baking powder
2 teaspoons soda
1½ teaspoons salt
1 cup brown sugar, firmly packed
3 cups sour milk or buttermilk
4 tablespoons salad oil
1½ cups chopped pecans

Stir unsifted whole-wheat flour into sifted flour, baking powder, soda, and salt. Sift together. Stir in brown sugar. Add sour milk or buttermilk and salad oil; stir smooth. Add pecans. Pour into 2 well-greased loaf pans. Bake in a moderate oven (350°) about 80 minutes.

Makes 2 loaves.

QUICK PECAN BANANA BREAD

¾ *cup sugar*
1 *egg*
½ *cup milk*
1 *cup mashed bananas* (3 *to* 4 *fully ripe*)
¾ *cup chopped pecans*
3 *cups prepared biscuit mix*

Mix together sugar, egg, milk and mashed bananas. Stir in pecans. Add biscuit mix; blend well. Turn into greased 9½×5¼×2¾-inch loaf pan. Bake in a moderate oven (350°) 45 to 50 minutes. Cool on rack.

Makes 1 loaf.

PECAN HONEY BUNS

1 *package dry yeast*
¼ *cup lukewarm water*
¼ *cup milk*
¼ *cup sugar*
½ *teaspoon salt*
¼ *cup shortening*
1¾ *cups sifted flour*
1 *egg*
1 *cup currants*
¼ *cup chopped pecans*
2 *teaspoons caramel syrup*

Soften yeast in lukewarm water. Scald milk. Add sugar, salt and shortening. Cool to lukewarm. Add 1 cup of the flour and beat well. Add softened yeast and egg; beat well. Cover. Add remaining ¾ cup flour to make a thick batter.

Beat thoroughly until smooth. Let rise until double (about 1 hour). Stir down and add currants.

Into greased, fluted muffin pans place caramel syrup; sprinkle chopped pecans on glaze. Drop batter by spoonfuls into pans, filling half full. Let rise until double (about 45 minutes). Bake in a moderately hot oven (375°) 24 to 30 minutes.

Makes 8 buns.

PECAN WAFFLES

2 cups sifted flour
3 teaspoons baking powder
¼ teaspoon salt
¾ cup chopped pecans
2 eggs, separated
1½ cups milk
6 tablespoons shortening, melted

Sift together dry ingredients and add pecans. Beat egg yolks until light; combine with milk and melted shortening and add to dry ingredients, mixing just until smooth. Beat egg whites until stiff and fold into batter. Bake in hot waffle iron.

Makes 6 to 8 waffles.

PECAN CHRISTMAS MERINGUES

2 egg whites
1 cup sugar
⅛ teaspoon salt
1 tablespoon lemon juice
1½ cups ground pecans
Maraschino cherries

Beat egg whites until stiff but not dry. Gradually add sugar and salt with lemon juice. Beat until mixture is very stiff. Remove ⅓ cup of the meringue; reserve. Fold pecans into remaining meringue. Drop by tablespoons on baking sheets covered with heavy brown paper. Top with small amount of reserved meringue. Decorate with small pieces of maraschino cherry. Bake in very slow oven (275°) 35 minutes.

Makes 3½ dozen cookies.

PECAN SNOWBALLS

¾ cup butter
½ cup sugar
1 egg
2 teaspoons vanilla
2 cups sifted flour
½ teaspoon salt
2 cups ground pecans
Confectioners' sugar

Cream butter. Add sugar gradually and cream well. Stir in egg and vanilla; beat until light and fluffy. Sift together flour and salt; add to creamed mixture with pecans; mix thoroughly. Shape into balls about ⅔ inch in diameter. Place on ungreased baking sheets. Bake in a moderate oven (350°) 20 minutes. Cool slightly on baking sheet; roll in sifted confectioners' sugar.

Makes approximately 7 dozen cookies.

CHOCOLATE PECAN BROWNIES

½ cup sifted flour
½ teaspoon baking powder
¼ teaspoon salt
1 6-ounce package (1 cup) semi-sweet chocolate morsels
⅓ cup shortening
2 eggs
½ cup sugar
1 teaspoon vanilla
1 cup chopped pecans

Sift flour, baking powder and salt together. Place semi-sweet chocolate and shortening in top of double boiler and melt over hot water. Mix until smooth and remove from hot water. Place eggs and sugar in mixing bowl and beat until thick and lemon-colored. Stir in dry ingredients. Add chocolate mixture and vanilla and stir until well blended. Pour into 8-inch square pan which has been greased and lined with greased wax paper. Sprinkle pecans over top and press lightly into batter. Bake in a moderately hot oven (375°) 25 minutes. Remove from pan, cool and cut into 2-inch squares.

Makes 16 brownies.

PECAN VIENNA COFFEE CAKE

TOPPING:

1 cup sifted flour
¾ cup light brown sugar, firmly packed
4 teaspoons cinnamon
½ cup butter or margarine
2 cups chopped pecans

Combine flour, sugar, cinnamon and butter or margarine blend until mixture is crumbly. Add pecans; mix well.

CAKE:

4 cups sifted flour
4 teaspoons baking powder
1 teaspoon salt
1 cup butter or margarine
1¾ cups granulated sugar
3 eggs
1 cup milk
1 teaspoon vanilla or lemon extract

Sift together flour, baking powder and salt. Cream butter or margarine and sugar. Add eggs, one at a time, and beat after each addition until light and creamy. Add dry ingredients alternately with milk and flavoring, blending well after each addition. Divide batter equally among 3 greased 9-inch round cake pans. Cover each evenly with an equal amount of topping. Bake in a moderate oven (350°) until done and browned, 30 to 35 minutes.

Makes 3 9-inch coffee cakes.

PECAN DEVIL'S FOOD CAKE

1½ cups sifted cake flour
1¼ cups sugar
½ cup cocoa
1¼ teaspoons soda
1 teaspoon salt
⅔ cup shortening
1 cup buttermilk
1 teaspoon vanilla
2 eggs, unbeaten
½ cup chopped pecans

Sift dry ingredients together into mixing bowl. Add shortening and buttermilk and vanilla. Mix 200 strokes by hand or 2 minutes by electric mixer at low speed. Scrape from sides of bowl while mixing. Add eggs and beat 100 strokes or 1 minute on electric mixer. Add pecans and beat 100 strokes or 1 minute on electric mixer. Pour into 2 greased 8-inch cake pans and bake in a moderate oven (350°) 30 minutes. Frost as desired.

Makes 2 8-inch layers.

BANANA PECAN CAKE

½ cup shortening
1½ cups sugar
2 eggs
¾ cup mashed bananas
2 cups sifted cake flour
¼ teaspoon baking powder
¾ teaspoon soda
½ teaspoon salt
¼ cup buttermilk
1 teaspoon vanilla
¾ cup chopped pecans

Cream shortening. Add sugar gradually; cream well. Add eggs one at a time, beating thoroughly after each addition. Add bananas. Sift together flour, baking powder, soda and salt. Add alternately with buttermilk to which vanilla has been added. Stir in pecans. Pour into 2 greased 9-inch cake pans and bake 30–35 minutes in a moderate oven (350°). Remove from pans and cool. Spread whipped cream between layers and on top and sides of cakes.

Makes 2 9-inch layers.

PECAN CHOCOLATE TORTE

6 eggs, separated
½ teaspoon salt
1 teaspoon vanilla
¾ cup sugar
1 cup sifted flour
1 cup finely chopped pecans
Chopped pecans for topping

Combine egg yolks, salt and vanilla; beat until very light and lemon-colored. Beat ½ cup of the sugar in gradually;

continue beating until very light and fluffy (about 5 minutes at medium speed). Stir in flour and the 1 cup of finely chopped pecans. Beat egg whites until they form soft peaks; beat in remaining ¼ cup sugar gradually and continue beating until glossy. Fold into egg yolk mixture.

Divide batter equally between 3 greased and floured 8-inch layer pans. Spread just enough to level. Bake in a slow oven (300°) until done, 20 to 25 minutes; remove from pans and cool thoroughly on rack.

Put layers together with chocolate creme filling, using ⅓ of filling on each layer. Sprinkle top with chopped pecans. Chill in refrigerator until filling is firm. Scrape excess filling off of torte. Cover sides of torte with Chocolate Satin Frosting. Chill and serve.

Makes 8 to 10 servings.

CHOCOLATE SATIN FROSTING

1 *cup sugar*
¼ *cup cornstarch*
¼ *teaspoon salt*
1 *cup boiling water*
2 *squares unsweetened chocolate, melted*
3 *tablespoons butter or margarine*

Combine sugar, cornstarch and salt in saucepan; mix well. Add water gradually, stirring constantly during addition. Place over low heat and cook until smooth and thickened, stirring constantly. Add chocolate and butter or margarine

Continue cooking and stirring until smooth and thick. Chill over ice water until cool and thick enough to spread; stir frequently during cooling. Spread sides of torte with frosting

PECAN SPICE CAKE

2 cups sifted cake flour
½ teaspoon salt
1 teaspoon baking powder
½ teaspoon soda
½ teaspoon ginger
1 teaspoon cinnamon
½ teaspoon nutmeg
½ teaspoon allspice
1 cup brown sugar
½ cup shortening
¾ cup buttermilk
2 eggs
½ cup chopped pecans

Sift flour, salt, baking powder, soda, and spices together into mixing bowl. Add sugar, shortening, and buttermilk. Beat 200 strokes or 2 minutes in electric mixer at low speed, scraping the bowl frequently. Add eggs and beat 100 strokes or 1 minute. Pour into 2 greased 8-inch cake pans and bake in a moderate oven (350°) 30 minutes. Remove from pan. When cool, ice with Orange Pecan Frosting.

Makes 2 8-inch layers.

ORANGE PECAN FROSTING

¼ cup butter
2 cups sifted confectioners' sugar
1 egg yolk, beaten
2 tablespoons orange juice
1½ teaspoons grated orange rind
½ cup chopped pecans

Cream butter. Gradually add 1 cup of the sugar while beating constantly. Add remaining sugar alternately with egg yolk which has been beaten and blended with orange juice and rind. Spread on cooled cake. Sprinkle pecans on top of cake.

SOUTHERN PECAN PIE

1 cup sugar
½ cup corn syrup
¼ cup butter, melted
3 eggs, well beaten
1 cup pecan halves
1 unbaked 9-inch pie shell

Mix sugar, syrup, and butter. Add eggs and pecans. Fill unbaked pie shell with mixture and bake in a hot oven (400°) 10 minutes. Reduce heat to moderate (350°) and continue baking 30–35 minutes.

Makes 1 9-inch pie.

PECAN SOUR CREAM PIE

1 unbaked 9-inch pie shell
1 cup broken pecans
2 teaspoons flour
¼ teaspoon cinnamon
¼ teaspoon cloves
1 cup sour cream
2 eggs, well beaten
1 cup sugar
½ teaspoon grated lemon rind

Line a pie plate with pastry and sprinkle it with pecans. Make custard by mixing flour, cinnamon, cloves and a little sour cream, gradually adding balance of sour cream. Stir in eggs, sugar and lemon rind.

Pour mixture into pie shell and place in hot oven (450°), lowering temperature control immediately to 325°. Bake until filling is firm, about 40 minutes. Serve either warm or cold, with whipped cream.

Makes 1 9-inch pie.

HONEY PECAN PIE

3 eggs
⅓ cup granulated sugar
⅓ cup light brown sugar
¼ teaspoon salt
¼ cup butter, melted
½ cup honey
½ cup white corn syrup
1 teaspoon vanilla
1 cup pecan halves
1 unbaked 9-inch pie shell

Beat eggs, mix in all other ingredients except pecan halves and pour into pastry-lined 9-inch pie pan. Arrange pecan halves on filling in desired pattern. Bake in a moderately hot oven (375°) 40 to 50 minutes until filling is set and pastry is golden brown. Cool. Serve cold or slightly warm.

Makes 1 9-inch pie.

BUTTER PECAN ICE CREAM

½ cup chopped pecans
3 tablespoons butter
1½ tablespoons cornstarch
½ cup sugar
2 tablespoons dark brown sugar
1 cup milk
1 teaspoon vanilla
1 cup heavy cream

Toast pecans in butter in skillet. Mix cornstarch and sugars. Add milk and cook over direct heat until thick, stirring constantly. Remove from heat; add vanilla. Chill. Whip cream until stiff. Fold in chilled mixture and pecans. Pour into freezing tray of automatic refrigerator and freeze.

Makes 6 servings.

PECAN PRALINES

1¾ cups sugar
⅛ teaspoon salt
1 cup water
1 tablespoon butter
¼ teaspoon maple flavoring
1 cup pecan halves

Melt ½ cup of the sugar in a skillet over low heat, stirring constantly, until sugar forms a pale-yellow syrup. Remove from heat and let stand 5 minutes. Add salt, water, and remaining sugar. Stir carefully until caramel is dissolved. Add butter and cook to soft-ball stage (236°), stirring constantly. Remove from heat. Let cool about 5 minutes. Add flavoring and pecans and stir until mixture becomes creamy. Drop by teaspoonfuls onto wax paper.

Makes about 1 pound.

PINE NUTS

THE PINE NUT

The name pignolia or pine nut is generally used to describe indiscriminately the seeds of many different species of pine tree.

In Italy and France the seeds of the Stone pine have been used for centuries, and we find the *pinocchi* (corrupted to pignolia) mentioned in the works of nearly all the ancient authors. The Stone pine with its flat, wide-spreading top is easily recognizable and is a familiar characteristic of the Riviera landscape. Its cones, 4 to 6 inches long, grow singly or in groups of two or three. Each cone contains about 100 turpentine-tasting nuts which are white or cream-colored, soft, and about the size of puffed rice. They are effective when used in making puddings, cakes, and confections including a type of marzipan. They may be eaten raw, roasted, salted, etc. and make a tasty dessert when served with a little lemon juice. Pine nuts are very rich in food value and extremely easy to digest.

Here in America the value of the piñon, a small low-growing tree commonly found on dry slopes and hills from Colorado to Texas, was early known to the Indians and Mexicans, who gathered the nuts of the pine to store for winter use when other food supplies became scanty. The most famous of the half-dozen American species is the Digger pine, which bears massive cones up to 10 inches long and weighing 4 pounds each. These cones may remain on the tree as long as seven years. Indian braves procured their food supply by climbing high into the trees to throw the matured cones down to squaws, who waited below.

Pine kernels were frequently ground and mixed with other foodstuffs. In modern days they have been highly favored by vegetarians as a substitute for suet.

Today, when we look about us, we see this source of food, once essential to the winter existence of the American Indian, lying wasted and undisturbed on the ground. Perhaps then it is well to re-establish our knowledge, our respect and our ability to profit from the nutritional value and tastiness of the fruit of the pine.

BROILED FILLETS WITH PINE NUT SAUCE

6 *fish fillets (about 1½ pounds), fresh or frozen*
2 *tablespoons melted butter or margarine*
Salt
Paprika

Wash fillets and wipe with cloth. Place fish on well-greased broiler rack or in shallow pan. Brush with melted butter, sprinkle with salt and paprika. Broil 2 inches from heat about 10 to 15 minutes, until brown. Serve with Pine Nut Sauce.

Makes 6 servings.

PINE NUT SAUCE

¼ *cup butter or margarine*
½ *cup sliced pine nuts*
2 *tablespoons lemon juice*

Melt butter over low heat. Add pine nuts and cook slowly 5 minutes or until butter is slightly browned. Add lemon juice; heat.

Makes 6 servings.

SAUSAGE PINE NUT SCRAMBLE

12 link sausages
½ cup pine nuts
6 eggs, slightly beaten
⅓ cup evaporated milk
¾ teaspoon salt
⅛ teaspoon hot pepper sauce
2 tablespoons minced parsley

Place sausage links in cold skillet with 2 tablespoons water. Simmer 5 minutes, covered. Drain and brown on all sides over low heat, uncovered, for about 12 minutes. Remove links, keeping them hot. Meanwhile grind pine nuts, using medium blade of food chopper. Combine with eggs, evaporated milk, salt and hot pepper sauce. Remove all but 2 tablespoons sausage drippings from skillet. Stir egg mixture into remaining drippings. Cook slowly until set, stirring occasionally. Correct seasonings. Pile on hot platter, sprinkle with chopped parsley and circle with browned sausage links.

Makes 4 servings.

CHICKEN PINE NUT PILAF

2½ cups chicken broth
1 cup uncooked rice
1 teaspoon salt
¼ cup chopped onions
½ cup diced celery
½ cup chopped pine nuts
1½ cups chopped cooked chicken

Bring chicken broth to a boil in a covered skillet or saucepan. Sprinkle the rice in slowly. Add salt, onions, celery, pine nuts and chicken. Cover and simmer about 25 minutes or until rice is soft and has absorbed the broth.

Makes 4 servings.

BAKED PINE NUT BEEF SANDWICH

1 cup ground cooked beef
⅓ cup chopped salted pine nuts
1 tablespoon finely chopped onions
2 tablespoons catchup
2 tablespoons mayonnaise
8 slices bread
3 eggs, slightly beaten
1 teaspoon salt
2 cups milk

Mix together the ground beef, pine nuts, onions, catchup and mayonnaise. Make 4 sandwiches with this mixture and the 8 slices of bread. Place in a baking dish. Pour over it the eggs, salt and milk, well blended. Bake in a moderate oven (350°) 1 hour.

Makes 4 sandwiches.

PINE NUT ONION PUFF

4 large sweet onions, sliced
1 cup grated process American cheese
1 cup pine nuts, chopped
¼ cup flour
½ teaspoon salt
2½ cups milk
3 eggs, well beaten

Separate sliced onions into rings. Boil in water 5 minutes. Remove onions from water and place in alternate layers with cheese and pine nuts in a buttered 1½-quart casserole. Blend the flour, salt, milk and well-beaten eggs together with a rotary beater until smooth. Pour this mixture over the onions, cheese and pine nuts. Bake in a moderate oven (350°) 40 minutes.

Makes 4–6 servings.

SWEET-POTATO NUTBURGERS

2 cups hot cooked mashed sweet potatoes
½ cup chopped pine nuts
¼ cup sugar
½ teaspoon cinnamon
1 cup finely ground pine nuts
¼ cup butter or margarine

Mix thoroughly the mashed sweet potatoes, chopped pine nuts, sugar and cinnamon. Shape into 8 flat patties. Roll in the ground pine nuts. Place on greased baking sheet and dot with butter or margarine. Bake in a hot oven (400°) 15 to 20 minutes or until nuts are toasty brown.

Makes 4 servings.

PINE NUT POTATO CAKES

1 cup chopped pine nuts
2 cups mashed white potatoes
½ teaspoon salt
2 tablespoons finely chopped onions
1 egg
Butter for frying

Combine all ingredients except butter. Shape into 8 flat cakes about ½ inch thick. Brown on both sides in butter in a heavy skillet.

Makes 4 servings.

PINE NUT BANANA BREAD

⅓ cup shortening
⅔ cup sugar
2 eggs
1 cup chopped pine nuts
1 cup mashed bananas (3 to 4 fully ripe)
1¾ cups sifted flour
2 teaspoons baking powder
¼ teaspoon soda

Cream shortening and sugar. Add unbeaten eggs one at a time, and beat thoroughly (one minute, medium speed with electric beater). Add the chopped pine nuts. Add the mashed bananas alternately with the flour, baking powder and soda which have been sifted together twice. Mix lightly, being careful not to overbeat. Turn into a greased 8½×4½×2½-inch loaf pan. Bake in a moderate oven (350°) about 70 minutes or until done.

Makes 1 loaf.

PINE NUT PIE

1 cup coarsely chopped pine nuts
1 unbaked 9-inch pie shell
1½ cups white corn syrup
4 eggs, slightly beaten
1 teaspoon vanilla
Dash of nutmeg

Spread pine nuts in the bottom of the unbaked pie shell. Mix thoroughly the corn syrup, slightly beaten eggs and vanilla. Pour over the nuts in the pie shell; add a dash of nutmeg if desired. Bake in a moderate oven (350°) 45 minutes.

Makes 1 9-inch pie.

PINE NUT DEVIL'S FOOD CAKE

¼ cup shortening
2 cups brown sugar, firmly packed
2 eggs
4 squares (4 ounces) unsweetened chocolate, melted
½ cup finely chopped pine nuts
2 cups sifted cake flour
2 teaspoons baking powder
½ teaspoon soda
½ teaspoon salt
1 cup plus 2 tablespoons milk
1 teaspoon vanilla

Cream shortening; add sugar gradually and cream thoroughly. Add eggs, one at a time, and beat until light and fluffy. Add melted chocolate and beat well. Mix in pine nuts. Sift together flour, baking powder, soda, and salt; add flour mixture alternately with milk to batter. Stir in vanilla. Pour into 2 deep, greased 8-inch layer pans and bake in a moderate oven (350°) 35 to 40 minutes. Let stand 5 minutes, then remove from pan. Cover with Glossy Chocolate Frosting or 7-minute frosting and garnish with pine nuts.

Makes 1 layer cake.

GLOSSY CHOCOLATE FROSTING

3 *squares* (3 *ounces*) *unsweetened chocolate, melted*
1¾ *cups sifted confectioners' sugar*
3 *tablespoons hot water*
3 *egg yolks, unbeaten*
¼ *cup butter or margarine*

Pour melted chocolate into mixing bowl. Add sugar and water; mix well. Add egg yolks, one at a time, beating well after each addition. Drop 1 tablespoon of butter at a time into the mixture and mix thoroughly.

PINE NUT CLUSTERS

1 6-*ounce package semi-sweet chocolate bits*
½ *cup sweetened condensed milk*
1 *cup pine nuts*

Melt chocolate bits over hot water on very low heat. Remove from heat and add the sweetened condensed milk and pine nuts. Drop by teaspoonfuls onto wax paper. Chill thoroughly.

Makes about 1 pound.

PISTACHIOS

THE PISTACHIO

Historically the pistachio nut, growing largely in the warmer parts of Asia, has been to the nomad what the pine nut has been to the American Indian. Valuable and important as a part of the winter nourishment when other foods were not plentiful, this small green kernel incited men to jealousy of forest rights and blood feuds of long duration.

The pistachio grows in hilly or mountain regions with poor, stony soils, under dry and adverse conditions. Heat is essential for the proper ripening of these nuts.

Male and female brownish green flowers are borne on different trees, and under cultivation it is essential that some male trees be planted in the groves to insure proper fertilization. (Interestingly enough, unfertilized flowers bear nuts which are hollow inside and devoid of kernels though outwardly they appear to be quite normal.)

The olive-like fruit of the pistachio grows in heavy grapelike clusters from trees reaching a height of about 25–30 feet and an age of about 300 years. The green husks of the fruit shrivel and yellow as they ripen around the single nuts they contain. The husks are rich in tannin and are used in the East for dying and tanning purposes. The nut, which cracks open spontaneously when it is ripe, is marketed both shelled and unshelled. Frequently it is fried in butter and served hot or roasted and hawked in the streets as a confection.

Popular in legend, the pistachio was long the symbol of happiness and plenty for lovers who met beneath its branches on moonlight nights, and it was known to be the favorite of the Queen of Sheba. Today the crops from Turkey, Iran, Afghanistan, Italy, and Southwestern United States supply us with the same luscious green meat—that from which we make the most desirable confections and ice creams and which we enjoy plain, in salted mixtures and as the "green almond" in decorating our most attractive-looking foods.

CREAM OF POTATO AND PISTACHIO SOUP

4 medium potatoes
1 small onion
4 cups water
2 tablespoons butter
2 tablespoons flour
1 teaspoon salt
2 cups milk
½ cup chopped pistachios
1 teaspoon chopped parsley

Boil potatoes and onion until tender in water. Remove potatoes and onion. Reserve water. Mash potatoes with butter, flour and salt. Add milk to 2 cups of reserved water. Bring to boil. Stir in potatoes while boiling. Remove from heat. Add pistachios. Place pinch of parsley in each plate. Pour over parsley and serve.

Makes 4 to 6 servings.

PISTACHIO PINEAPPLE SPARERIBS

2 pounds spareribs
½ cup flour
2 teaspoons salt
⅓ cup salad oil
1 can (1 pound 14 ounces) sliced pineapple
1 tablespoon vinegar
2 tablespoons brown sugar
2 tablespoons water
1 small onion
1 green pepper
½ cup water
2 tablespoons flour
2 teaspoons soy sauce
2 teaspoons catchup
½ cup chopped pistachios

Cut spareribs into 1-inch sections, roll in flour and sprinkle with salt. Brown spareribs in hot oil. Pour off excess oil. Drain juice from pineapple and mix with vinegar, brown sugar, and the 2 tablespoons water; add to spareribs. Cut each pineapple slice into 8 pieces, quarter the onion, and cut green pepper into 1-inch squares. Add these to spareribs, cover, and simmer 45 minutes. Make a smooth paste of the ½ cup of water, flour, soy sauce, and catchup. Remove spareribs from pan, stir flour paste into drippings and cook until slightly thickened. Pour over spareribs and sprinkle with chopped pistachios.

Makes 4 servings.

CURRIED TURKEY WITH PISTACHIOS

¼ cup butter or margarine
4 tablespoons flour
2½ cups milk
½ teaspoon salt
½ teaspoon paprika
¼ teaspoon pepper
¼ teaspoon curry powder
1 bay leaf
2 cups diced cooked turkey
1 cup pistachios
1 cup cooked peas

Melt butter or margarine in a 2-quart saucepan and blend in flour. Scald milk; gradually pour into saucepan while stirring. Add salt, paprika, pepper, curry powder and bay leaf. Stirring constantly, simmer until thick. Remove bay leaf. Mix in turkey, pistachios and peas. Heat thoroughly. Serve on buttered toast or hot cooked rice. Garnish with parsley.

Makes 6 servings.

PISTACHIO AND POTATO MOLD

1 envelope unflavored gelatine
¼ cup cold water
1 3-ounce package lemon-flavored gelatine
¼ teaspoon salt
2 tablespoons vinegar
1½ cups hot water
2 cups cooked diced cold potatoes
1½ teaspoons salt
1 tablespoon minced onions
3 tablespoons chopped pimiento-stuffed olives
½ teaspoon celery seed
Pepper to taste
½ cup mayonnaise or salad dressing
1 cup pistachios

Soften unflavored gelatine in cold water. Dissolve lemon gelatine, ¼ teaspoon salt, vinegar and softened unflavored gelatine in very hot water. Chill until partially congealed. Meanwhile toss together lightly the potatoes, 1½ teaspoon salt, onions, olives, celery seed and pepper. Fold in mayonnaise and pistachios. Turn chilled gelatine mixture into a deep bowl and whip with rotary egg beater until smooth and fluffy. Fold in potato mixture. Pour into 5-cup mold or individual molds. Chill overnight or until very firm. Unmold on serving plate. Garnish with parsley or chicory sprays.

Makes 6 to 8 servings.

PISTACHIO FRUIT GELATINE SALAD

1 3-ounce package pineapple-flavored gelatine
¼ teaspoon salt
1½ cups hot liquid (drained pineapple juice and boiling water)
2 teaspoons lemon juice
1 3-ounce package cream cheese, softened
½ cup mayonnaise or salad dressing
1 cup crushed pineapple drained
½ cup maraschino cherries, sliced
⅓ cup finely chopped pistachios

In a bowl dissolve pineapple gelatine and salt in combined hot water and pineapple juice. Add lemon juice, cream cheese and mayonnaise. Whip with rotary egg beater until well blended. Chill until partially congealed. Whip with egg beater until fluffy. Fold in well-drained pineapple, cherries and pistachios. Pour into 1-quart mold or individual molds. Chill overnight or until very firm. Unmold on crisp lettuce or watercress.

Makes 6 servings.

PISTACHIO RICE STUFFING

1 *cup uncooked wild rice, washed and drained*
1 *cup uncooked white rice*
1 *large onion, chopped*
1 *cup sliced celery*
2 *tablespoons butter or margarine*
⅓ *cup chopped pistachios*
⅓ *cup finely chopped parsley*
½ *teaspoon curry powder*
½ *teaspoon dried sweet basil*
1½ *teaspoons salt*
½ *teaspoon pepper*
¼ *teaspoon monosodium glutamate*

Cook wild rice and white rice according to package directions. While rice is cooking, sauté onion and celery in butter or margarine until tender; then combine with the cooked wild rice and white rice. Add pistachios, parsley, curry powder, basil, salt, pepper and monosodium glutamate. Mix together well.

Makes 6 cups stuffing.

PISTACHIO HONEY RING

¼ *teaspoon ginger*
¼ *cup honey*
1 *8-ounce can refrigerated oven-ready biscuits*
⅓ *cup chopped pistachios*

Blend ginger and honey. Roll each biscuit to 4 inches in diameter. Spread biscuit with honey mixture; sprinkle with chopped nuts. Roll biscuit in shape of cornucopia, with nuts thickest in wide end. Pinch points to seal. Arrange rolled biscuits side by side in circle in 8-inch pie pan, points inward. Brush with melted butter. Bake in moderately hot oven (375°) 20–25 minutes. Turn out of pan.

Makes 10 rolls.

PISTACHIO NUT PRALINE COOKIES

⅔ cup butter or margarine
1 cup sugar
½ cup unsulphured molasses
2 eggs
½ teaspoon vanilla
1¾ cups sifted flour
½ teaspoon soda
¼ teaspoon salt
2 cups chopped pistachios

Melt butter slowly in saucepan large enough for mixing dough. Cool; stir in sugar and molasses. Add eggs and vanilla; beat well. Sift together flour, soda and salt; gradually add to first mixture. Stir in chopped pistachio nuts. Drop by level teaspoonfuls 2 inches apart on ungreased baking sheets. Bake in moderately hot oven (375°) 8 minutes. Cool slightly (about 12 minutes) before removing from baking sheet.

Makes 15 dozen 2-inch cookies.

PISTACHIO LEMON LOGS

½ cup butter
½ cup shortening
¾ cup brown sugar, firmly packed
¼ teaspoon salt
1 teaspoon finely grated lemon rind
1 tablespoon lemon juice
2½ cups sifted flour
1 cup chopped pistachios

Cream butter, shortening and sugar together. Add salt, lemon rind, lemon juice, and flour; mix well. Chill dough until stiff. Shape into finger lengths. Roll in chopped pistachios. Bake on ungreased cooky sheet in a hot oven (400°) 10 to 12 minutes.

Makes 3–4 dozen cookies.

PISTACHIO PIE

3 eggs
⅔ cup sugar
½ teaspoon salt
⅓ cup melted butter or margarine
1 cup dark corn syrup
1 cup pistachios
1 unbaked 9-inch pie shell

Beat eggs thoroughly with sugar, salt, melted butter and syrup. Add pistachios. Pour into unbaked 9-inch pie shell. Bake in moderate oven (350°) 50 minutes, or until knife inserted into center of filling comes out clean.

Makes 1 9-inch pie.

PINEAPPLE PISTACHIO PIE

¼ cup butter or margarine
½ cup brown sugar, firmly packed
2 tablespoons flour
1 teaspoon vanilla
¼ teaspoon salt
3 eggs, beaten
1 cup dark corn syrup
1 cup chopped pistachios
1 can (1 pound 4 ounces) pineapple tidbits, well drained
1 unbaked 9-inch pie shell

Cream thoroughly butter, sugar, flour, vanilla and salt. Blend in eggs and corn syrup. Fold in pistachios and pineapple. Pour into pie shell. Bake in a moderate oven (325°) 45 minutes or until firm.

Makes 1 9-inch pie.

PISTACHIO CARAMEL ROLL

¼ cup butter
3 cups sifted confectioners' sugar
⅛ teaspoon salt
¼ teaspoon rum flavoring
2 tablespoons hot milk
1 cup brown sugar, firmly packed
2 tablespoons butter
¼ cup milk
1 tablespoon corn syrup
¼ cup toasted chopped pistachios
1 (½ pound) package caramels (28 caramels)
1–2 tablespoons water
1 cup sliced pistachios

Cream together the butter, confectioners' sugar, salt and rum flavoring. Stir in hot milk; beat until creamy and smooth. Combine brown sugar, butter, milk and corn syrup. Cook, stirring occasionally, until mixture reaches firm ball stage (248°–250°). Pour over first mixture, beating until smooth and thick. Pour out on buttered platter. When set and easy to handle, knead in the chopped pistachios and form into two rolls. Chill. Heat caramels with water in top of double boiler. Spread caramel mixture on top side of roll. Press on sliced pistachios. Turn roll over, spread with more caramel and sliced nuts. Repeat process for other roll. Chill; slice.

Makes 2¼ pounds of candy.

WALNUTS

THE WALNUT

California walnuts come from beautiful trees growing along our West Coast which have been developed over the years. They are descendants of the Persian walnut, regarded by some to be the most important nut grown.

From earliest times the nuts have been known to be native to Persia and were thus called *Persicon* by the Romans, who received knowledge of their delicacy from the Greeks and held the walnut in such high esteem as to consider it food fit for the Gods, calling it "the nut of Jupiter." Ovid tells us that these nuts were thrown amongst the children during Roman weddings by the bride and groom to symbolize their leave-taking of childish amusements. Magic healing powers were attributed to the oils and elixirs made from its leaves, shells and kernels, and the Roman legionnaires carried the nuts with them to England, where they became numerous in parks and gardens until the beginning of the last century, when the demand for the wood of this tree—which achieves a height of 60 feet and a spread of 40–50 feet—became so fashionable that they were indiscriminately cut down and sold.

The walnut tree bears lovely flowers of both sexes, the stamens taking an entire year to develop. The flowers are in full bloom in May before the large spreading top of the tree is in full leaf. Small green fruits about the size of a plum appear in July. These fruits turn brown and split, disclosing nuts which are exceedingly rich in food value.

During two thousand years of continuous cultivation and selection the Persian walnut has so greatly changed in character and habit that it is beyond short description here, but it is significant to say that today its identity has become submerged in its current appellation, the "California walnut." At the present time walnut orchards cover some 122,000 acres of California, which has the proper soil and proper weather conditions to allow for cultivation, irrigation, pruning, and spraying of these trees.

Cooperative research and development have furthered the work of the first orchardists, who consulted on walnut culture with the early Franciscan fathers, who made plantings in the yards of their missions. The first commercial producer, Joseph Sexton, made his first planting in 1867 from seeds of the Persian walnut that he later developed into the Placentia variety. In 1871 French-born Felix Gillet established a nursery from which emerged the famous Franquette, still produced on 30 percent of today's bearing acreage.

Harvest time in California lasts from mid-September to mid-November; the nuts are gathered by both hand and machine methods. Some of the nuts must be hulled; this job is done by machine. After being washed, the nuts are submitted to a mechanical dehydration process which dries them thoroughly enough to prevent any deterioration. Then the walnuts are sized according to government specification as large, medium or babies, and are weighed, sorted, bleached and packaged for market.

About 60 percent of the crop goes to in-shell consumer demands. These walnuts will keep from 18 to 24 months as long as there has been no detriment to the protective brown covering on the kernel of the nut, called the pellicle. In the case of shelled nuts a pellicle substitute has been developed which treats the kernels and protects them from rancidity. Continuous sampling and analysis of in-shell walnuts and walnut kernels as they are prepared for market assure today's consumer of receiving the highest quality at all times.

Walnuts contain a high proportion of unsaturated fatty acids and are a good source of iron and vitamin B. They are delicious in cookies, cakes, pies, candy, bread, casseroles, salads, and in the traditional nut bowl. Plain, they combine perfectly with cheese, fruit, wine, and chocolate, and are a useful and decorative snack before and after dinner and as a between-meal appetite appeaser.

CHINESE CHICKEN AND WALNUTS

1 medium onion, sliced
1 green pepper, cut in strips
3 tablespoons butter
2 to 3 cups coarsely cut cooked chicken or turkey
1 3-ounce can mushrooms
1 cup sliced celery
2 tablespoons cornstarch
2 cups rich-flavored chicken broth
½ cup chablis or other white table wine
Dash of white pepper
2 to 3 tablespoons soy sauce
1 cup toasted walnut halves or pieces

Cook onion and green pepper in butter 2 or 3 minutes. Add chicken, and drained mushrooms (save their liquid). Cook slowly about 10 minutes. Add celery. Mix cornstarch with ¼ cup of the cold broth. Add rest of broth, wine, and mushroom liquid to chicken mixture. When this is hot, stir in cornstarch and broth and cook, stirring gently, until sauce is bubbling hot and looks clear. Add pepper, and soy sauce to taste. Let cook slowly 5 to 10 minutes longer, until slightly thickened. Stir in the toasted walnuts. Serve with hot, fluffy steamed rice.

Makes 6 servings.

DEVILED CRAB GOURMET

2 cups cooked crab meat
½ cup toasted walnuts, coarsely chopped
2 hard-cooked eggs, diced
½ cup mayonnaise
2 teaspoons lemon juice
1 teaspoon Worcestershire sauce
¼ teaspoon dry mustard
¼ teaspoon salt
Dash of cayenne
1 cup buttered bread crumbs

Flake crab meat, toss with walnuts and eggs; mix mayonnaise with lemon juice, Worcestershire and seasonings and add. Spoon into baking shells or small shallow baking dish. Cover with buttered crumbs. Bake in a hot oven (400°) about 20 minutes until golden brown. Top each serving with a sprig of parsley.

Makes 4 servings.

GLORIOUS FRUIT SALAD

1 large orange
2 medium-sized bananas
1½ cups halved seeded grapes
½ cup chopped walnuts
¼ cup heavy cream
1 tablespoon lemon juice
1 tablespoon sugar
Few grains salt
Lettuce cups

Peel and dice orange. Peel and slice bananas. Add grapes and walnuts. Whip cream until stiff and blend in lemon juice, sugar and salt. Pour over fruit-walnut mixture and blend lightly. Serve in lettuce cups.

Makes 4 to 6 servings.

OLD FAVORITE WALNUT BREAD

3 cups sifted flour
1 cup sugar
4 teaspoons baking powder
1½ teaspoons salt
1 cup chopped walnuts
1 cup raisins or chopped dates (optional)
1 egg
1¼ cups milk
2 tablespoons melted shortening

Sift first 4 ingredients into bowl. Add walnuts and raisins or dates. Beat egg with fork, add milk and melted shortening. Stir into flour mixture and beat with spoon until well blended. Bake in greased 9×5×3-inch loaf pan in moderate oven (350°) 60 to 70 minutes or until done when tested.

Makes 1 loaf.

CHOCOLATE WALNUT JUMBOS

2 cups walnut halves
¼ cup soft butter or margarine
½ cup sugar
1 egg
1½ teaspoons vanilla
1½ squares unsweetened chocolate, melted
½ cup sifted flour
¼ teaspoon baking powder
½ teaspoon salt

Put walnut kernels in a paper or plastic bag, crush with rolling pin to break them coarsely. Stir together butter, sugar, egg, and vanilla; beat with spoon just until smooth. Stir in melted chocolate, then flour sifted with baking powder and salt. Stir in walnuts. Drop by teaspoonfuls on greased baking sheet. Bake in a moderate oven (350°) 10 minutes. Cookies should still be soft when taken from oven. Cool on rack.

Makes about 30.

DIAMOND GEMS

½ cup butter
2 tablespoons sugar
⅛ teaspoon salt
1 teaspoon vanilla
1 cup sifted flour
1 cup very finely chopped walnuts
Confectioners' sugar

Cream butter with sugar till fluffy. Add salt and vanilla. Work in flour gradually. Stir in walnuts. Chill. Form teaspoonfuls into shape of small walnut. Bake on ungreased cooky sheet in a moderate oven (350°) 15 to 17 minutes. Cool 3 minutes, then roll in confectioners' sugar. Cool on rack. Dust tops of cookies again with powdered sugar.

Makes 3½ dozen rich cookies.

JUST RIGHT OATMEAL COOKIES

½ cup shortening
1 cup sugar
1 egg, unbeaten
⅓ cup buttermilk
1 cup sifted flour
½ teaspoon salt
½ teaspoon soda
½ teaspoon baking powder
½ teaspoon nutmeg
½ teaspoon cinnamon
1¼ cups rolled oats
¾ cup chopped walnuts
½ cup raisins or chopped dates

Cream together shortening and sugar. Beat in egg. Add buttermilk. Stir in flour sifted with salt, soda, baking powder, and spices. Add rolled oats, walnuts, and raisins or dates. Drop by teaspoonfuls 2 inches apart on ungreased baking sheet. Bake in a hot oven (400°) 9 to 12 minutes until lightly browned.

Makes 30 to 36.

CHOCO-WALNUT DROPS

1 *cup plus 2 tablespoons sifted flour*
½ *teaspoon soda*
½ *teaspoon salt*
½ *cup sugar*
¼ *cup brown sugar, firmly packed*
1 *egg, unbeaten*
1 *teaspoon vanilla*
½ *cup shortening, part butter*
½ *cup chopped walnuts*
1 *cup (6-ounce package) semi-sweet chocolate pieces*

Sift flour, soda, salt, and sugar into mixing bowl. Add brown sugar, egg, vanilla, and shortening. Stir with spoon about a minute, until well mixed. Add walnuts and chocolate pieces. Drop by small spoonfuls about 2 inches apart on ungreased baking sheet. Bake in a moderately hot oven (375°) 10 to 12 minutes.

Makes about 50.

PINEAPPLE DROP COOKIES

1 *cup light brown sugar, firmly packed*
½ *cup mixed shortening and butter*
1 *egg, unbeaten*
1 *teaspoon vanilla*
¾ *cup crushed pineapple, drained*
2 *cups sifted flour*
1 *teaspoon baking powder*
½ *teaspoon soda*
½ *teaspoon salt*
¾ *cup chopped walnuts*
½ *cup raisins*

Stir together sugar, shortening, egg, and vanilla until blended. Add pineapple. Stir in sifted dry ingredients, then walnuts and raisins. Drop by heaping teaspoonfuls on ungreased baking sheet. Bake in a moderately hot oven (375°) about 12 minutes until lightly browned.

Makes 3 dozen.

WALNUT FEATHER CAKE

½ cup sifted flour
¼ teaspoon mace
¼ teaspoon cloves
2 cups walnuts grated, ground or very finely chopped
7 eggs, separated
1 cup sugar
2 teaspoons lemon juice
Rind of one lemon, finely grated
¾ teaspoon cream of tartar
½ teaspoon salt

Line removable bottom of 10-inch tube pan with wax paper. Sift flour, mace, cloves over walnuts; mix. Beat egg yolks till thick; add sugar very gradually, beat thoroughly (10 to 15 minutes). Beat in lemon juice, rind. Clean beaters, beat egg whites until frothy; add cream of tartar, salt. Continue beating till firm peaks will form. Heap walnut mixture on top of yolks; add whites. Fold together only till blended. Bake in a slow oven (325°) 45 minutes, or until cake tests done. Invert pan. Cool at least 1 hour. Serve unfrosted, or mix powdered sugar and orange marmalade for glaze.

Makes 1 cake.

POTATO CHOCOLATE CAKE

1 cup hot unseasoned mashed potatoes
2 cups sugar
⅔ cup shortening
4 eggs, unbeaten
1 teaspoon vanilla
2 cups sifted flour
½ cup cocoa
3 teaspoons baking powder
1 teaspoon each cinnamon and nutmeg
½ teaspoon salt
½ cup milk
1 cup chopped walnuts

Line bottoms of two 9-inch layer pans or a 13×9×2-inch oblong pan with wax paper cut to fit. Prepare mashed potatoes. (Easy way: follow directions "for 2 servings" on package mashed potatoes.) Measure; set aside. Gradually beat sugar into shortening, until fluffy. Add eggs one at a time, beating well. Add vanilla and potatoes. Add sifted dry ingredients and milk alternately, about ¼ of each at a time, beating smooth. Stir in walnuts. Bake layers in a moderate oven (350°) 40 to 45 minutes, loaf about 50 minutes, or until done when tested. Let stand 5 minutes. Turn out on racks, peel off paper. When cool, frost with butter-cream or other frosting and sprinkle thickly with additional walnuts.

Makes 1 oblong loaf or 1 layer cake.

BUTTER-CREAM FROSTING

Gradually beat 1 pound (4 cups) confectioners' sugar into ½ cup soft butter or margarine, adding 3 to 4 tablespoons cream or milk as needed to make right consistency. Add 1½ teaspoons vanilla. For chocolate butter-cream frosting, melt 3 squares unsweetened chocolate and blend with butter before adding sugar.

Makes enough for a 2-layer or loaf cake.

PLYMOUTH CHESS PIE

½ cup butter or margarine
1 cup sugar
4 eggs
¼ cup heavy cream
1 teaspoon grated lemon rind
1 teaspoon lemon juice
1 teaspoon vanilla
1 cup chopped walnuts
1 cup seedless raisins
Unbaked 9-inch pie shell with high fluted edge

Cream butter with sugar. Beat in, one at a time, 3 whole eggs and 1 yolk. Stir in cream, lemon rind and juice, and vanilla. (Mixture will look like cottage cheese.) Add walnuts and raisins. Beat egg white stiff and fold in. Pour into unbaked crust and bake in a moderate oven (350°) 40 to 45 minutes until golden brown.

Makes 1 9-inch pie.

WALNUT FESTIVAL PIE

2 eggs
1 cup dark corn syrup
1 teaspoon vanilla
1 tablespoon melted butter
½ cup sugar
1 tablespoon flour
¼ teaspoon salt
1 cup chopped walnuts
Unbaked 8-inch or 9-inch pie shell

Beat eggs with fork. Add corn syrup, vanilla, and butter. Mix sugar, flour, and salt and add. Stir in walnuts. Pour into unbaked shell. Bake in a moderately hot oven, (375°), 40 to 50 minutes. Test by inserting tip of knife in filling: when it comes out clean, pie is done. Serve cold.

Makes 7 or 8 servings.

HOLIDAY PUMPKIN CHIFFON PIE

½ cup brown sugar, firmly packed
1 envelope unflavored gelatine
½ teaspoon salt
½ teaspoon cinnamon
½ teaspoon ginger
½ teaspoon nutmeg
¾ cup milk
1¼ cups canned pumpkin
3 eggs, separated
½ cup sugar
¾ cup chopped walnuts
1 baked 9-inch pie shell

Mix brown sugar, dry gelatine, salt and spices in saucepan. Stir in milk, pumpkin, and egg yolks. Cook over low heat, stirring constantly, about 5 minutes, until bubbling. Cook 1 minute longer, stirring. Chill until cold and fairly stiff. Beat egg whites until foamy; gradually beat in sugar; beat very stiff. With same beater, beat pumpkin mixture about 2 minutes, until light and fluffy. Add walnuts. Fold at once into meringue, and heap in baked pie shell. Chill 3 hours or longer. Top with sour cream or whipped cream and decorate with walnuts halves or pieces.

Makes 1 9-inch pie.

CRACKER MERINGUE TORTE

2 *egg whites*
⅛ *teaspoon salt*
½ *teaspoon vanilla*
½ *cup sugar*
½ *cup soda-cracker crumbs*
½ *cup coarsely chopped walnuts*
½ *teaspoon baking powder*

To egg whites add salt and vanilla; beat until beginning to mound. Gradually beat in sugar, making a very stiff meringue. Fold in cracker crumbs mixed with walnuts and baking powder. Spoon into buttered 8-inch pie pan; bake in a slow oven (325°) about 30 minutes, until firm to touch and lightly browned. Cool in pan. Serve with sweetened whipped cream, decorated with walnuts. Or fill with sweetened fresh or frozen berries or peaches, or with lemon pie filling or instant pudding; chill. Top with whipped cream and chopped walnuts. Cut like a pie.

Makes 1 8-inch pie.

WALNUT GOLDEN GLOW

1 *cup apricot pulp (fresh, canned, or cooked dried)*
1 *teaspoon lemon juice*
2 *egg whites*
Dash of salt
½ *cup sugar*
½ *cup chopped walnuts*

Mix apricot pulp and lemon juice. Beat egg whites with salt to soft fluff; gradually beat in sugar, making stiff meringue. Fold in fruit and walnuts. Spoon into sherbet glasses. Garnish with whipped cream and a few walnut pieces.

Makes 5 or 6 servings.

DIAMOND PLUM PUDDING

Stir together in large bowl:

1 cup chopped walnuts
3 cups raisins
1½ cups currants
⅓ cup finely cut citron
⅓ cup glacé orange, cut fine
⅓ cup glacé lemon peel, cut fine
Grated rind and juice of 1 lemon
⅓ cup cider

In second bowl mix these ingredients:

1 cup sifted flour
1¼ cups fine dry bread crumbs
1 cup brown sugar, firmly packed
1 teaspoon salt
1 teaspoon nutmeg
2 cups suet, finely chopped or ground

Add these to contents of first bowl; mix well. Add ½ cup milk and 4 beaten eggs; blend thoroughly. Pack lightly into a greased 2-quart mold. Cover with lid or foil. Set on rack in deep kettle, pour in boiling water to half the depth of mold. Cover kettle and boil steadily 5 to 6 hours. Add more boiling water as needed.

Remove from mold to cool, then wrap in foil; refrigerate until used. Resteam for an hour and serve hot, flaming or not, with Holiday Hard Sauce.

Makes 12 or more servings.

HOLIDAY HARD SAUCE

Blend 2 tablespoons hot water with ½ cup soft butter or margarine. Gradually add 3 cups or more sifted confectioners' sugar; beat until fluffy. Beat in 1 teaspoon vanilla and, if you like, 2 to 3 tablespoons sherry, rum or brandy, plus a little more confectioners' sugar. Add ½ cup chopped and well-drained maraschino cherries. Drop by spoonfuls on wax paper. Chill.

PEACH OR APPLE CRISP

- *3 to 4 cups sliced peaches or apples (or a 1-pound 4-ounce can sliced peaches, drained)*
- *1 tablespoon lemon juice*
- *½ cup flour*
- *½ cup brown sugar*
- *¼ teaspoon salt*
- *¼ teaspoon each nutmeg and cinnamon*
- *¼ cup soft butter or margarine*
- *½ cup chopped walnuts*

Spread fruit in shallow baking dish or pie pan; sprinkle with lemon juice. Mix flour, sugar, salt, and spices; work in butter till crumbly; add walnuts. Spread mixture evenly over fruit. Bake in a moderately hot oven (375°) 30 to 40 minutes, or until crust is brown and fruit tender. Serve warm with ice cream or plain cream.

Makes 5 servings.

WON'T FAIL FUDGE

- *⅔ cup (1 small can) evaporated milk*
- *16 marshmallows, or a 5–10-ounce jar marshmallow cream*
- *1⅓ cups sugar*
- *¼ teaspoon salt*
- *¼ cup butter*
- *1½ cups semi-sweet chocolate pieces*
- *1 teaspoon vanilla*
- *1 cup coarsely chopped walnuts*

Mix first five ingredients in saucepan. Stirring constantly, heat to boiling; boil 5 minutes. Remove from heat. Add chocolate and stir until melted. Stir in vanilla and walnuts; spread in buttered 8-inch pan. Cool until firm.

Makes about 2 pounds.

DATE WALNUT CHEWS

- 1 *cup sugar*
- 1 *teaspoon baking powder*
- ¾ *cup sifted flour*
- ¼ *teaspoon salt*
- 1 *cup chopped pitted dates*
- 1 *cup finely chopped walnuts*
- 2 *eggs, beaten*

Sift sugar, baking powder, flour and salt into bowl. Stir in dates and walnuts. Add eggs; mix thoroughly. Spread in a greased 15½×10½×1-inch jelly-roll pan. Bake in a moderately hot oven (375°) about 18 minutes. Cut into 1½-inch squares while warm. Roll in powdered sugar.

Makes about 5 dozen.

WALNUT RUM BALLS

- 3 *cups finely rolled vanilla wafers*
- 1 *cup confectioners' sugar*
- 1½ *tablespoons cocoa*
- 1½ *cups finely chopped walnuts*
- 3 *tablespoons corn syrup*
- ½ *cup rum or bourbon*

Mix all ingredients together; shape into 1-inch balls and roll in confectioners' or granulated sugar. Good to eat right away or later! Store in tight container.

Makes about 40.

DIAMOND DIVINITY

2 cups sugar
½ cup light corn syrup
½ cup water
⅛ teaspoon salt
2 egg whites
1 teaspoon vanilla
1 cup chopped walnuts

Mix sugar, corn syrup, water and salt in saucepan. Heat slowly until sugar is dissolved; then boil gently without stirring to 240°, or until a few drops in cold water form a firm soft ball. While syrup boils, beat egg whites stiff. Beating constantly, slowly pour about a third of the hot syrup over them. Put rest of syrup back to cook to 265°, hard-ball stage. Gradually beat this syrup into egg whites, add vanilla, and continue beating until mixture will just hold its shape. Add walnuts. (If weather is damp and candy refuses to hold its shape, beat in 1 teaspoon powdered sugar at this stage.) Drop from teaspoon onto wax paper or pour into buttered pan.

Makes about 2 pounds.

INDEX